96

6

1997

97

1997

'

TUTANKHAMUN: HIS TOMB AND ITS TREASURES

TUTANKHAMUN: HIS TOMB AND ITS TREASURES

TUTANK

HIS TOMB AND

LONDON·1979

HAMUN:
ITS TREASURES

I.E.S. EDWARDS
Former Keeper of Egyptian Antiquities at the British Museum

VICTOR GOLLANCZ LTD

ISBN 0 575 02714 2

Harry Burton's black and white photographs,
made in the course of the excavation of the tomb,
were printed from the original glass negatives
by the Metropolitan Museum's Photograph Studio.

Photographer's Note: Every photographic exercise
of this nature and scope involves contributions,
often spontaneous, by several persons. My
appreciation is expressed in this instance to
Christine Roussel, Christine Lilyquist, Ken Kay,
Richard Morsches, and William Pons.
Lee Boltin
Cairo and New York
November 1975 – March 1976

Originally published in the United States by
The Metropolitan Museum of Art and Alfred A.
Knopf, Inc., New York.

Editor: Katharine Stoddert Gilbert
Designer: Alvin Grossman

Printed in Italy by A. Mondadori Editore

FOREWORD
THOMAS HOVING
DIRECTOR
THE METROPOLITAN MUSEUM OF ART

Since the discovery of Tutankhamun's tomb and its sumptuous contents, found in November 1922 by Howard Carter acting under the patronage of Lord Carnarvon, there have been many books written about the young pharaoh, his tomb in the barren Valley of the Kings, and the unparalleled works of art in those four diminutive rooms. But there has been no book like this, for **Tutankhamun: His Tomb and Its Treasures** is the first book deliberately planned as a step-by-step trip through the richly furnished funerary chambers of a pharaoh who lived during one of the most splendid periods of ancient Egypt.

This book presents the fascinating archaeological record of the exploration of the tomb in original black and white photographs taken by Harry Burton, the expedition's photographer, who captured the cluttered magnificence of each room as a whole as well as closeups of objects both precious and mundane: ranging from touching mementos of the pharaoh's boyhood to the magnificent jewelry, furniture, and sculpture that accompanied him to the afterlife. These are juxtaposed with masterful color photographs by Lee Boltin, made, by special permission of the Cairo Museum, under ideal conditions never before granted.

This unusual counterpoint of modern and historic photographs reveals the excitement of discovery and the splendor of the finds: the dazzling, puzzling piles of objects as, one by one, the rooms are explored; the achingly slow uncovering of the mummy with its precious ornaments in the hot, cramped Burial Chamber; the first glance after 3,200 years into a chest crammed with jewelry.

In a way this book, sensitively written by the Egyptologist I. E. S. Edwards, is a time machine, reaching back not only to the fabulous discovery in 1922 but thousands of years to the time when ancient robbers made their sacrilegious visitations to the tomb, and then earlier, to that moment when the mourners placed a tiny wreath of flowers on the coffin and then sealed – for eternity, they believed – the tomb of the young god-king.

WHO WAS TUTANKHAMUN?

Tutankhamun, born in about 1343 B.C., was probably a son of the famous pharaoh Akhenaton by a minor wife. His probable brother or half-brother, Smenkhkara, was chosen by Akhenaton in about 1336 B.C. as co-regent and heir apparent, a position to which he was entitled through his marriage to his half-sister, Meritaton, the eldest surviving daughter of Akhenaton and Nafertiti. The death of both kings some two years later resulted in the accession of Tutankhaton, as Tutankhamun was then called, when he was about nine years old and married to Ankhesenpaaton, Meritaton's younger sister.

Akhenaton had imposed on his subjects a monotheistic creed, proclaiming Aton, the god in the sun's disk, the only god. He had also built a capital at Amarna to replace Thebes and had introduced a new style in art. Opposition to his innovations, already apparent before his death, led Tutankhaton, in about the third year of his reign, to reopen the temples of the older gods, which Akhenaton had closed, to restore the capital to Thebes (Luxor), and to signify the return to favor of the former state god Amun by changing his own name to Tutankhamun and his wife's to Ankhesenamun. He died at the age of about nineteen in about 1325 B.C.

Tutankhamun's tomb lies in a deep gorge in the rocky desert west of the Nile opposite Luxor, the so-called Valley of the Kings. The first king to be buried there was Thutmose I (about 1524 to 1518 B.C.), whose architect, Ineny, recorded that he constructed the rock-hewn tomb "in a solitary place where no one could watch and no one could listen." Earlier kings had built massive pyramids, but here nature had provided a ready-made pyramid of rock, 1,650 feet high (shown in this picture), which dominated the whole Valley. Little could Ineny have imagined that his secluded place would become the royal necropolis for the next four hundred and fifty years. The only practicable approach to the Valley lay along the ravine shown in this photograph, and through it must have passed Tutankhamun's funeral procession and all the treasures which went with him to his tomb.

Between 1903 and 1912 an American businessman named Theodore M. Davis financed a series of excavations in the Valley of the Kings, the work being supervised by experienced Egyptologists, one of whom was Howard Carter. Many important discoveries were made, including four royal tombs, all robbed, and

the intact tomb of Yuya and Tuya, Tutankhamun's presumed great-grandparents, which yielded a wealth of funerary equipment without parallel at that time. Davis believed he had also found what had survived of Tutankhamun's funerary furniture: in reality it was a collection of objects stolen in antiquity and hidden by the robbers, but never reclaimed. Another discovery, made in 1907, was a collection of objects buried in the pit shown in the foreground at the left of this photograph. They seemed of little consequence, but time would show that they offered a vital clue to the location of Tutankhamun's tomb.

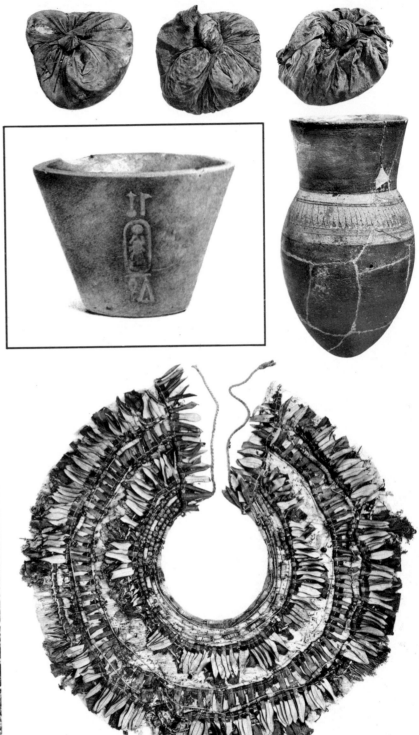

In January 1908 Herbert Winlock, a curator of the Egyptian Department in the Metropolitan Museum, visited Davis and studied the large pottery jars found in the pit and their contents, principally linen bags, some filled with natron, cloths (some dated to Tutankhamun's last years) and bandages, impressions of Tutankhamun's seal, broken pottery vessels, bones of birds and animals, and floral collars. Winlock realized that the natron and bandages were materials used in embalming Tutankhamun, which, being ritually unclean, were unfit to place in his tomb; the bones, vessels, and collars were relics of the feasts held at his funeral. Besides the objects in the pit and the cache, Davis found, under a boulder not far away, a blue faience cup bearing Tutankhamun's name.

In 1914, when Davis had completed his excavations, Lord Carnarvon was granted the concession to explore the Valley of the Kings. Howard Carter, who had directed Lord Carnarvon's excavations since 1907, was ready to begin immediately the search for Tutankhamun's tomb, but the First World War intervened and the project remained in abeyance until 1917. After five unsuccessful seasons Lord Carnarvon doubted whether further expense was justified, but he yielded to Carter's plea for one more season. Digging was resumed on November 1, 1922, and on the fourth morning, under a hut built by workmen when constructing the nearby tomb of Ramesses VI, the top step of a rock-cut staircase was uncovered. It was only a few feet from the spot where Carter had stopped digging in his first season in order not to prevent tourists from entering Ramesses VI's tomb. Could it lead to the tomb of Tutankhamun?

Overleaf: By the next afternoon, twelve steps had been cleared without reaching the bottom, but it was evident that the staircase ended in a rock-hewn doorway, blocked with boulders and coated with a layer of mud plaster. Before the plaster had dried, seals had been pressed against it, leaving impressions of a recumbent jackal over nine captives, like the one on the right in this group (found later on another door in the tomb), but without the cartouche: it was the seal used by the ancient necropolis inspectors responsible for guarding the tombs. Did it mean that he had found an unrobbed tomb? The identity of the owner still remained to be discovered. He made a small hole at the top of the doorway to see what lay beyond, but all he could see was a tunnel blocked from floor to ceiling.

The next morning Carter sent his historic cable to Lord Carnarvon: "At last have made wonderful discovery in the Valley: a magnificent tomb with seals intact; re-covered same for your arrival; congratulations." Many days must elapse before Lord Carnarvon could reach Egypt. Carter, as he stated in his cable, refilled the staircase. He had no photographer to record every event: these photographs, which show the doorway boarded up and men carrying baskets of limestone chips and sand to fill the staircase, were taken when he repeated the operation some weeks later. The method, however, was similar on both occasions, except that the stone blocking of the doorway made boarding unnecessary on the first occasion. It was laborious, but it gave the maximum protection and, at a time when a man was paid twenty-five cents a day (at the rate of exchange then prevailing), the cost was not appreciable.

Lord Carnarvon, accompanied by his daughter, reached Luxor on November 23. The staircase was again uncovered and four remaining steps were cleared, revealing the lower part of the blocked doorway. The seals on that part were different from those above; they were the seals of Tutankhamun, like the two left-hand examples already illustrated. It was now evident, however, that the blocking which bore the seals of the necropolis inspectors was not original but a replacement, whereas the part of the blocking with Tutankhamun's seals had never been disturbed. The tomb was certainly Tutankhamun's; it had been violated before the reign of Ramesses VI (about 1141-1133 B.C.), when the hut over the staircase was built, and its entrance had been reblocked by the necropolis staff. Its contents could hardly have survived intact, but the replacement of the blocking suggested that the thieves had left something valuable behind.

Behind the blocked doorway lay a sloping tunnel filled from floor to ceiling with sand and rubble. The removal of the filling resulted in another disconcerting discovery: mixed with the rubble were objects, some broken, which had almost certainly come from the tomb. One of these objects was a painted wooden lotus flower surmounted by a human head. It was a beautiful piece of sculpture, evidently a representation of Tutankhamun emerging from the lotus, just as the sun god had done when he came into existence from a lotus flower floating on the surface of the primordial ocean at the time of the creation of the universe. At the end of the tunnel was another blocked doorway, almost exactly like the first, which was soon to be replaced by the steel gate shown in this picture.

November twenty-sixth was what Carter later described as "the day of days, the most wonderful that I have ever lived through, and certainly one whose like I can never hope to see again." With his assistant, A. R. Callender, and Lord Carnarvon and his daughter, Lady Evelyn Herbert, waiting anxiously at his side, he made a small hole in the top of the blocking of the second doorway and inserted a candle through it. Gradually, as his eyes grew accustomed to the dim light, he was able to pick out "strange animals, statues and gold, everywhere the glint of gold." Immediately in front of him was a bed, its side in the form of a cow. Very probably the purpose of this bed was to convey Tutankhamun to the solar heaven. According to legend the sun god, at the end of his reign on earth, had ascended to the sky on the back of a cow goddess named Mehturt.

Overleaf: Lying inside the doorway was an alabaster chalice. Carter called it the king's wishing cup, because the inscription on the outer rim wished him "millions of years" happily enjoying the cool breeze from the north (i.e. the Mediterranean). The bowl represents an open white lotus. The handles represent a blue lotus and two buds surmounted by the god of eternity, Heh, holding in each hand the hieroglyphic sign for "life" and a notched palm rib–the sign for "year"–resting on a tadpole mounted on a ring of rope–the signs for "100,000" and "infinity." The whole group of signs expresses the wish that Tutankhamun's years may continue for 100,000 times infinity.

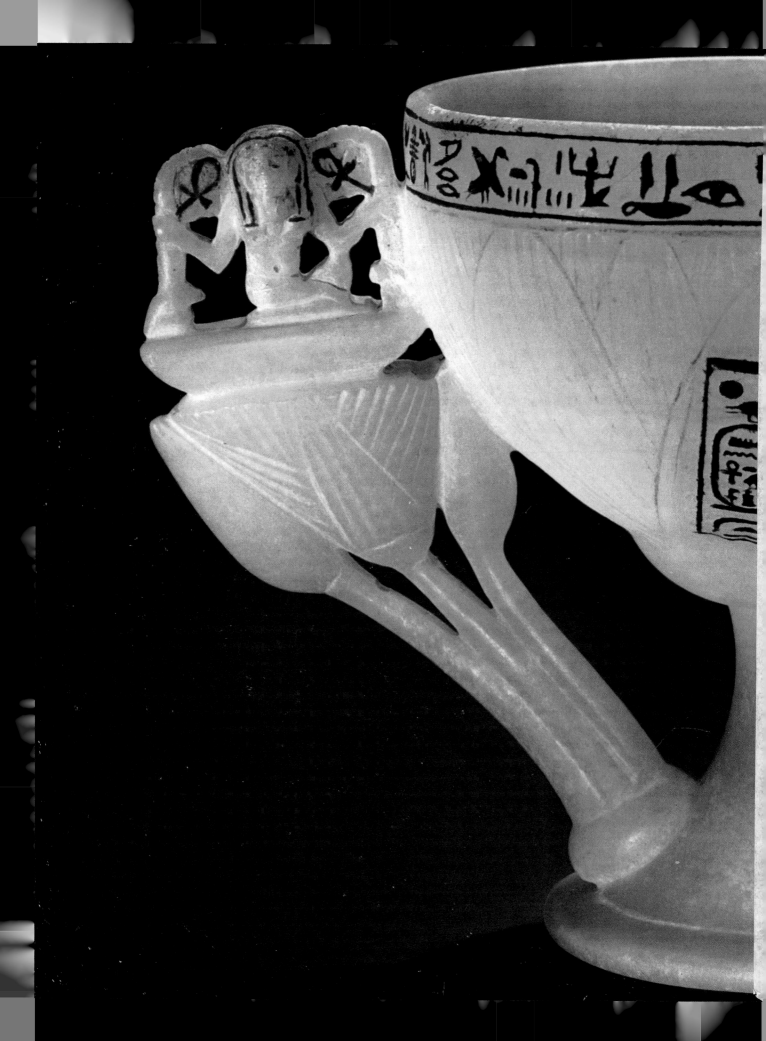

Between the cow-sided bed and one with lion sides were five ornamental perfume vases carved of alabaster. The vase on the left is made of two pieces cemented together, the lower representing a stand flanked by "life" signs, with human hands holding scepters symbolizing "dominion." The inner hands also hold papyrus flowers. Carved on the neck of the vase is a bust of the goddess Hathor, wearing a broad bead collar with pendent blue lotus and buds and a mandrake fruit. Tut-ankhamun's names are incised on the belly of the vase beneath a garland of lotus petals and two human breasts. Tied to the vase are stems of lilies (left) and papyrus flowers, the emblems of Upper and Lower Egypt, flanked by the hieroglyphic sign for "years" mounted on the signs for "100,000" and "infinity."

The size of this stout little chair (14½ inches wide) (illustrated overleaf) shows that it was made for a child, certainly Tutankhamun, or Tutankhaton, as he was called in his boyhood. Carter described the wood as ebony, a highly prized material imported from Africa. It is inlaid with ivory and the joints are riveted with copper or bronze pins capped with gold. The legs, carved like a lion's and having paws with claws of ivory, stand on beaded drums shod with metal. Other relics of the king's childhood were also found in the tomb; they may have been placed there for sentimental reasons or for his use after rebirth.

Pages 32-33: In contrast with the formal ornamentation of the back, naturalistic designs decorate the gilded panels of the armrests. Within a border of continuous spirals, the whole length of the field is occupied by a recumbent ibex. Being a desert animal, it is appropriate that a sprig of a desert plant should fill the space above the ibex's back.

Tutankhamun's tomb was too small to accommodate adequately what it contained, but very much of the disorder was undoubtedly caused by the ancient robbers. The security staff of the necropolis made access to it more difficult after the first robbery; their work in the inner chambers, however, was most perfunctory. In this picture of the southern half of the Antechamber (26 feet long by 12 feet wide), the largest objects visible are two overturned chariots, which were too large to bring into the tomb without being dismantled, a hippopotamus-headed bed, and the cow bed discussed earlier. A golden throne can be seen under the hippopotamus-headed bed. In the bottom right-hand corner is a pile of wooden food boxes, each of which bears an ink inscription naming its intended contents, but the actual contents seldom corresponded with what was written on the label. Nevertheless boxes with the same label generally contained the same wrong article.

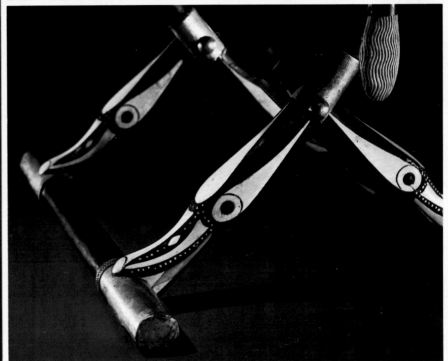

This stool can be seen in the preceding photograph, placed on the floor of the Antechamber between the two beds with animal sides. Its seat is an imitation of a leopard skin, made of ebony and inlaid with ivory spots and hollow rosettes. Representations of the paws were probably attached to the four corners of the overhang of the seat; if so, they were wrenched off by the ancient robbers, perhaps in order to obtain the gold from the claws. Owing to the color of the materials used, the markings are light and the background is dark, a reversal of the contrast in nature. The crossed legs are in the form of ducks' necks and heads holding the lower crossbars in their bills. Such legs were a common feature in Egyptian folding stools with flexible seats. In this model the seat is made of an inflexible material and is firmly joined to the legs, thus making the whole stool rigid. The legs and lower crossbars are embellished with gold bands bordered with fine granular work and the pivotal pins are capped with gold. At the tip of the tail, which seems disproportionately short, the individual hairs are marked in the ivory overlay.

Leopards, extinct in Egypt in Tutankhamun's time, were plentiful in Nubia and their skins were regularly sent as tribute to the pharaoh.

Of all the treasures in the tomb nothing, at the time of the discovery, stirred popular imagination more vividly than the golden throne. Its association with state occasions, which must have surpassed in magnificence anything staged elsewhere in the ancient world, was enough to vest it with an aura of romance. And yet its principal decoration was a representation of what appeared to be an intimate episode, a simple incident hardly appropriate for such a purpose. More than any other piece of furniture in the royal palace, the throne might have been expected to conform strictly with what convention ordained and tradition required. It clearly does so in every other respect, but the revolutionary changes in art and religion introduced by Akhenaton at Amarna were still too recent to be entirely discarded when Tutankhamun became king, and this scene is undoubtedly a relic from the immediate past.

The throne is made of wood and overlaid with sheet gold. Its lion-paw legs are mounted on beaded drums shod with copper or bronze. At the front of the seat are two heads of lions, symbolizing the eastern and western horizons, over each of which a lion was believed to stand as guardian. The space between the seat and the stretchers was used for the regular heraldic device of intertwined papyrus and lotus stems tied to the hieroglyphic sign for "unification," thereby commemorating the unification of Upper and Lower Egypt under one crown. The panels of the armrests are largely filled with winged cobras wearing the double crown and protecting the king's names with their wings.

Page 40: The scene carved on the inner panel is overlaid with gold and inlaid mainly with colored glass, faience, and translucent stone painted at the back. It is set in a pavilion bedecked with flowers and surmounted by an elaborate frieze topped by cobras with sun's disks. The king and queen, both wearing ceremonial crowns and garments of silver, are represented in the naturalistic style of Amarna art. Even more specifically recalling Amarna is the disk of the god Aton, identified by name, whose rays, each terminating in a human hand, shine on the royal pair through the open top of the pavilion. The queen is in the act of anointing the king with perfume from a vessel held in her left hand, very probably on the occasion of his coronation. Behind the queen is a large bead collar on a stand.

Made perhaps of the timber commonly called "cedar of Lebanon" (believed to be Cilician fir), this very elegant chair closely resembles the golden throne in the design of its lower part. The damage done to it by the ancient robbers is also very similar: the whole of the heraldic device commemorating the unification of Upper and Lower Egypt under one crown, which occupied the space between the seat and the stretchers, has been ripped off, with the exception of the hieroglyphic sign for unification in the middle of each side. On the back panel is a superbly carved figure of the god of eternity, Heh, with a "life" sign slung over his right arm and holding in each hand a notched palm rib, attached at the base to the sign for "100,000" mounted on a coil of rope. At the top of each palm rib is a solar disk and cobra from whose hood is suspended a banner inscribed with the king's Horus name. The inscriptions emphasize the divine origin of the king.

When the tomb was constructed it was probably not intended for the burial of a king. Space in it was too confined for working on the objects, apart from photographing them in situ, recording evidence which would be lost when they were moved, and preparing them for transfer to a field laboratory, which was established in the tomb of Sethy II at the end of the Valley. When these preliminary operations were completed, each object was placed on a wooden stretcher or tray and carried out of the tomb, accompanied by Carter himself and an armed military escort, for its journey to the laboratory. Tourists would wait for hours in the hope of witnessing one of these processions; whenever possible the objects were conveyed without covers so that people could see them. In this picture the painted wooden lifesize portrait bust of Tutankhamun shown on the right is being taken to the laboratory.

116

The chariot was introduced into Egypt from western Asia about three centuries before the time of Tutankhamun. Two dismantled state chariots were placed just inside the Antechamber. The body of each chariot is made of bentwood overlaid with thin sheet gold on gesso. One (upper left) is decorated with bands of embossed marguerites and continuous spirals, feather patterns, and floral designs, either embossed or inlaid with glass and semiprecious stones. A medallion near the base is inlaid with the eye of Ra and a cobra with solar disk. On the other chariot Tutankhamun is depicted as a sphinx, protected by the vulture of the goddess Nekhbet, trampling on bound Negro and Asiatic captives. In this chariot the medallion is inlaid with a gold boss surrounded by concentric circles of silver and colored glass.

The openwork gold buckle shows Tutankhamun in a chariot drawn by two richly caparisoned horses, accompanied by his hound and driving before him a Negro and an Asiatic captive. Similar bound captives are represented beneath the chariot in the heraldic device for the unification of Upper and Lower Egypt. Above and behind the king are his protectors, the vulture of Upper Egypt and the winged cobra of Lower Egypt.

Mounted on a trelliswork stand, in front of the hippopotamus bed, was a long box, made of wood, painted white, and of ebony. It contained clothes, bows, arrows, and sticks. The crook of the stick illustrated here is decorated with two very realistic effigies of bound captives, one a Negro and the other an Asian. The exposed parts of the Negro's body are modeled in ebony and those of the Asian, whose features are painted, are carved in ivory. Nothing is known about the purpose of the stick, but its appearance suggests that it had a ceremonial function.

The sides of this bed, made of
gilded wood, are composed
of parts of three animals: the
heads are those of hippopotami,
the bodies those of crocodiles,
and the legs those of lions.
An inscription on the mattress
describes Tutankhamun as
"beloved of Ammut," from
which it may be inferred that
the bed had some connection
with Ammut. A composite
creature named Ammut, meaning "Devourer of the Dead,"
is regularly depicted in the
Book of the Dead; its function
was to devour those whose
sins in life debarred them from
entering the kingdom of the
god Osiris after death. Ammut
is composed of parts of the
same animals as those of this
bed, but the parts are different:
it has a crocodile's head, fore-
part of a lion, and hindquarters
of a hippopotomus. Practical
considerations may have dic-
tated the different order in
the bed: the crocodile bodies,
being long, were the most suitable for the sides and lion
paws were more suitable than
those of a hippopotamus for
the legs. Nevertheless it is
strange that a creature with
Ammut's malevolent attributes
should have been chosen.

Made of wood and overlaid with sheet gold on a backing of plaster, this shrine is mounted on a sledge overlaid with silver. Architecturally it is a model of the ancient shrine of the vulture goddess of Upper Egypt, Nekhbet, called the Great House. The doors are fastened by silver bolts which slide through gold staples. Three objects were found inside the shrine: a gilded wooden pedestal with back plinth for a statuette (probably made of gold and stolen by the robbers), part of a corselet, and a bead necklace with a pendant representing a human-headed serpent, named the Great Enchantress, suckling Tutankhamun. On the outside of the shrine the king and queen are depicted, in the intimate style of Amarna art, engaged in various activities.

The king, seated on a folding stool covered with a leopard skin and cushion, pours water into the cupped hand of the queen, squatting on a hassock. By an artistic convention the left hands of both figures are shown as though

In this scene the queen, whose left forearm is disproportionately long, ties a floral collar around the king's neck. On her head is a crown of cobras with solar disks, surmounted by a cone of unguent in a holder and two larger

A more formal note is struck in the scene on the left, which may represent an episode in Tutankhamun's coronation ceremonies. The king is seated on a cushioned chair holding a vessel with flowers, into which the queen pours water. In her left hand she holds a bouquet composed of a blue lotus and bud and a poppy. In addition to his broad collar and a two-stringed torque the king wears a long necklace with broad straps, on which are suspended cartouches bearing his throne name, Nebkheperura, and his personal name, Tutankhamun.

Inside the shrine can be seen the pedestal and back plinth for a statuette. The pedestal still shows the imprint of the feet of the statuette.

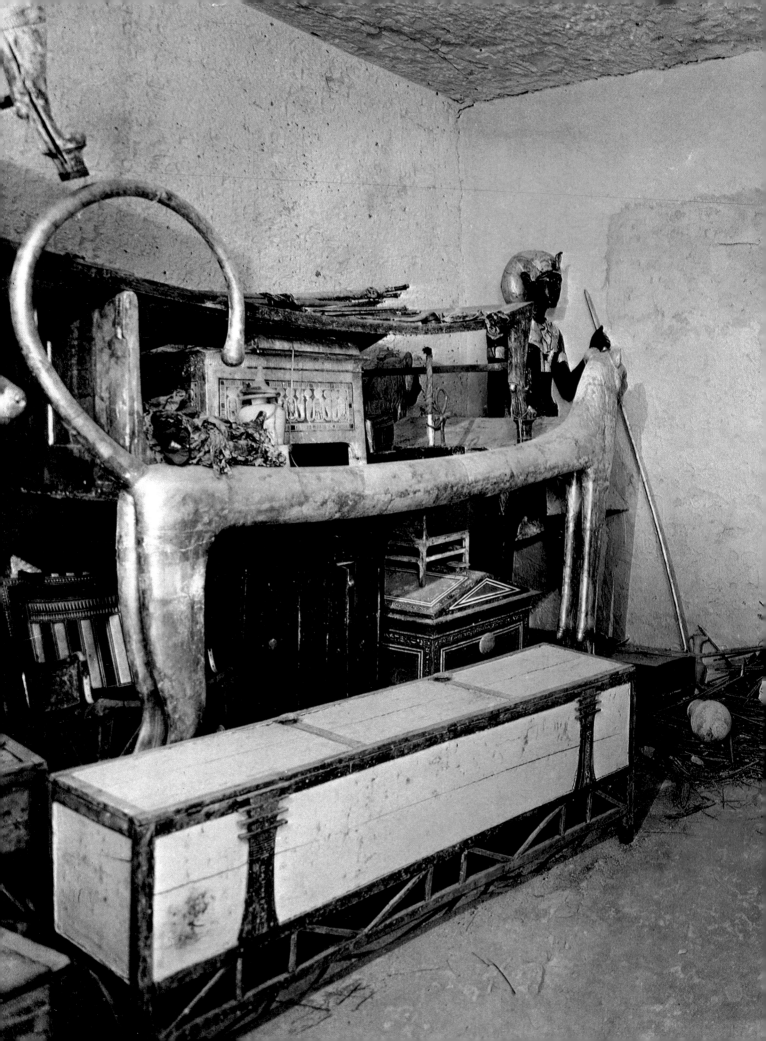

Writing about this bed ten years after its discovery, Carter expressed the opinion that the animals were cheetahs, and not lions as he had first supposed. His original identification, however, is broadly supported by evidence which he apparently overlooked. Like the two other animal-sided beds, it is made of gilded wood in four detachable units: the two sides, a mattress, and a wooden frame with sockets for dowels beneath the feet of the lions. The sides are joined to the mattress by hooks and staples. An inscription on the mattress names Mehturt as the deity represented by the lions (which may equally well be lionesses), but Mehturt was a cow goddess, not a lioness. A lioness goddess, Isis-Meht, is, however, named in the inscription on the cow bed and it seems clear that the two inscriptions were inadvertently transposed by the engraver. The animals on this bed probably therefore represent Isis-Meht, whose special functions are not known, and consequently the purpose of the bed is hard to determine. Nevertheless, beds of a similar form are depicted in scenes of royal births carved on temple walls and it may be inferred that this bed was part of the equipment intended for Tutankhamun's rebirth after death.

Overleaf: Although the animals which form the sides of this bed have been regarded as male, their heads and facial features are the same as those of a very commonly represented lioness goddess, Sekhmet. Each figure is carved of wood, overlaid with a thin layer of plaster and gilded. The nose and drops under the eyes are inlaid with blue glass. The painted eyes have lids of black glass.

It would be difficult to imagine a greater jumble of priceless treasures than can be seen in this photograph, and the confusion would be even worse if the diverse contents of the boxes were visible. The topmost object is an ebony bed with a woven cord mattress on which were laid bows, arrows, and staffs. Between it and the lion bed are placed a bundle of linen, a wooden casket with blue faience panels ornamented with gold, a ritual vase of alabaster, and three torch holders of bronze and gold, one with a torch of twisted linen still standing in the oil holder. On the floor, from left to right, are the child's chair shown earlier in this book, a painted alabaster casket, two black wooden shrines mounted on sledges, each of which contained a gilded snake on a standard (emblems of a district in middle Egypt), and a portable chest on the lid of which is a wooden object which may be a stand. Filling the gap between the portable chest and the wall are a footstool and blue faience vases, while a hassock lies on its side in front of the portable chest. Partly visible behind the lion bed is a small chest which had been robbed of all its contents except one stone armlet.

The most distinctive feature of this chest is the set of retractable carrying poles beneath its floor. Each pole slides backward and forward through two bronze rings mounted on pieces of board which are attached to the underside of the floorboards. A collar at the rear end of each pole, greater in circumference than the rings, prevents the pole from slipping forward through the back ring. When the chest was not being carried, the poles could be pushed back until they were entirely concealed from view.

Both the gable lid and the chest itself have frameworks of ebony and inner panels of a red wood, probably cedar, bordered by strips of ivory and ebony. The feet are capped with bronze shoes and strengthened with bent right-angle braces. At one end of the lid and beneath it, on the end wall of the chest, are mushroom-shaped knobs around which a string was tied and the knot sealed.

Carved in shallow relief under the lower knob are figures of the king offering to the god Onnophris (another form of Osiris) a lamp and a pot of perfume. On a stand between the two figures is a vase with a spout in the form of an ostrich plume in miniature. It was the hieroglyphic symbol for truth, justice, and right order. The original contents of the chest had been stolen by the robbers, and the necropolis staff had filled it with miscellaneous objects including stone knives, a lid of a rush basket, lumps of resin, balls of incense, and dried fruits.

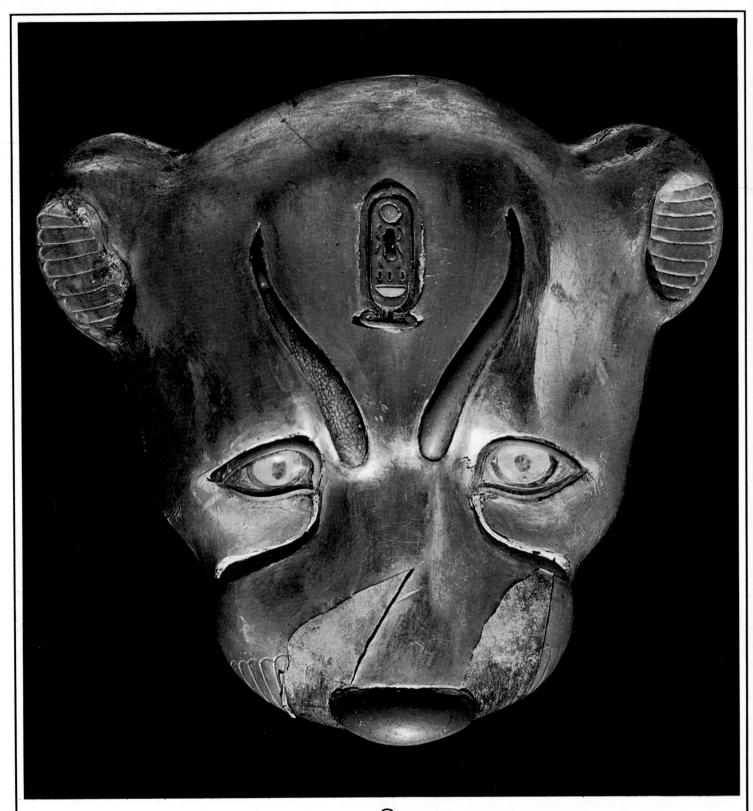

Some classes of Egyptian priests wore leopard-skin cloaks when performing their official duties; one class, the high priests of Heliopolis, wore such cloaks embellished with gold five-pointed stars, no doubt because their duties included the observation of the stars. Tutankhamun, who was in theory the high priest of every god, was buried with two priestly cloaks, one a real leopard skin and the other an imitation. Both were adorned with gold stars and both had heads made of wood. The head illustrated here belonged to the real skin. It is overlaid with gold and inlaid with colored glass. The eyes are painted behind translucent quartz. It was found in the casket on top of the lion bed.

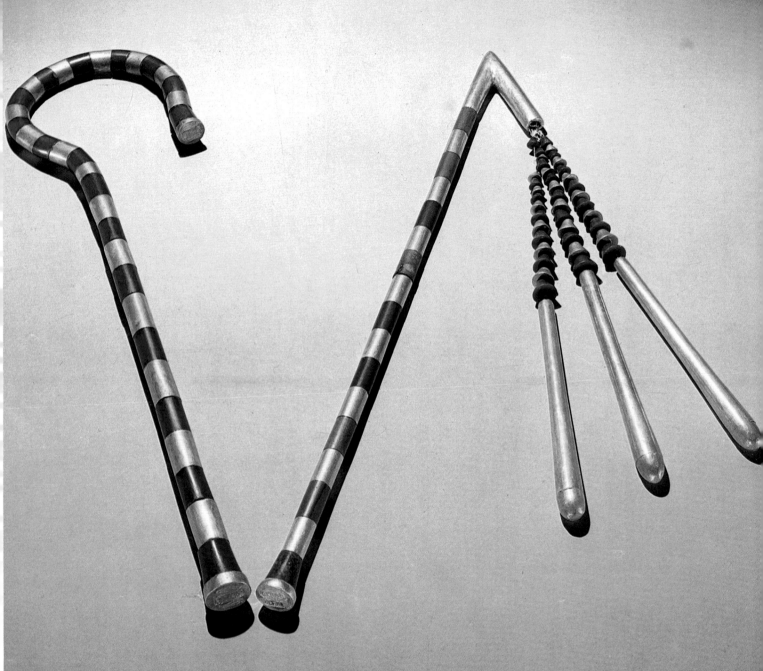

The crook and flail were the emblems
of the god Osiris, but they were also held by kings on certain ceremonial
occasions. This crook was found in the same box as the leopard's head, and
the flail in a casket in the Treasury. One of the ceremonies in which the king
held a crook and flail was the coronation; it is possible that the flail, at least,
was used in his first coronation at Amarna when he was about nine. It is
inscribed on the gold cap with his personal name in its early form, Tutankhaton, and also with the name which he received on ascending the throne,
Nebkheperura. The crook bears only his throne name.

One of the most surprising of the many remarkable objects packed in the same box as the
leopard's head and the crook was a linen scarf
which proved, on examination, to contain eight
solid gold finger rings. The cloth had been
twisted and knotted to form a small bag for them.
There could be no doubt that it was the ancient
robbers who had wrapped them up, but why they
had left them in the tomb was a mystery. Either
they had forgotten them or they were disturbed
and did not have time to collect all their loot.
It is a tribute to the honesty of the necropolis staff
that they resisted the temptation to purloin
them when they were repairing the damage done
by the robbers.

Incised and painted on the lid of this alabaster casket (overleaf) are two formal bouquets, separated by a column of inscription giving the king's names and titles. Each of the bouquets consists of a papyrus flower between two poppies, lotus petals, poppies, corn-flowers, and mandrakes. The knobs on both the lid and the box are made of volcanic glass (obsidian). Under the lower knob are the names and titles of Tutankhamun and queen Ankhesenamun. The casket, found beneath the lion bed, contained an ivory pomegranate, some cloth, animal hair, and two balls of hair wrapped in linen. The balls may have had a magical purpose or they may have sym-bolized some kind of contract.

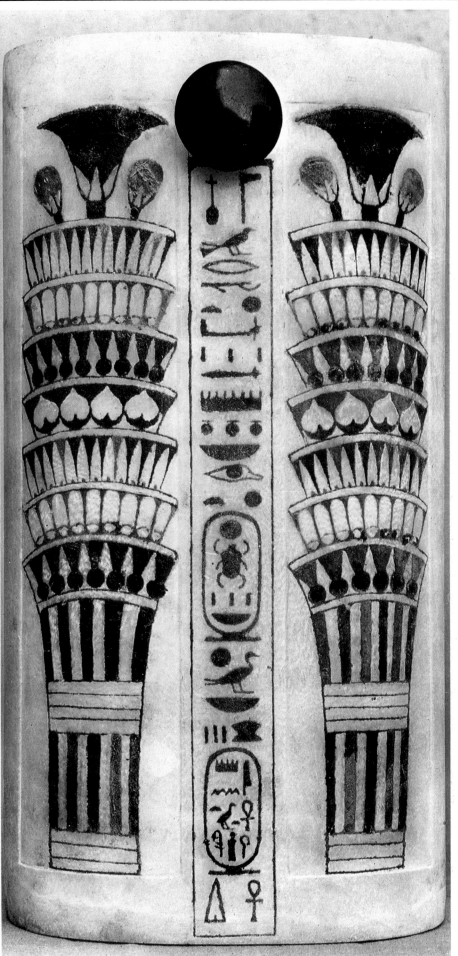

The trumpet, found in a wooden box near the lion bed, is made of bronze or copper and is partly overlaid with gold. On the bell are figures of Tutankhamun receiving the emblem of life from Amun, Ra-Harakhty (left), and Ptah (right). The bell of the wooden stopper is painted to represent an open lotus. It was used either with a cloth to clean the instrument or bare to preserve its shape. Egyptian trumpets had no valves and the mouthpieces were not cup-shaped. Employed chiefly on military occasions, they are the only ancient instruments of which the exact sound as heard by the ancients can be reproduced today.

The objects visible in this photograph of the northeast corner of the Antechamber, from left to right, are an alabaster vase, the painted chest, one of the wooden statues of the king, two funerary bouquets of leaves, a lid of a rush basket and a bundle consisting of reeds and papyrus matting, another alabaster vase, and a pottery vase under reed and other fragments.

Although the painted chest was probably intended to hold only the king's sandals, some fifty objects were found in it, including several sandals. They were, however, mainly articles of apparel: robes, shawls, collars, and an imitation leopard skin. The necropolis staff had stuffed them into the chest without paying any attention to order and tidiness. According to Carter, unpacking this one chest occupied him for three weeks.

Overleaf: As works of art, the scenes painted on the plaster overlay of this wooden chest are outstanding. They are traditional in their general character, probably done by the court painter for the pleasure of the king. In each scene, apart from the heraldic devices at the ends, the king is shown riding in his chariot, drawn by two richly caparisoned, lively steeds. The quarry in the two scenes on the lid is the fauna of the desert: lions, lionesses, wild asses, ostriches, a hyena, and antelopes. On the sides the victims are Nubians and Asiatics. The same foes, trodden underfoot by the king in the guise of a sphinx, are shown in the scenes at the ends of the chest. Particularly noticeable is the skill with which the artist has portrayed the agony of the victims, human and animal, and the naturalistic detail which he has introduced into the composition.

Two life-size statues of the king stood one on each side of the blocked doorway leading to the Burial Chamber. They are made of wood, varnished with black resin and embellished with gilded accouterments. A gilded mace is held in the right hand, and in the left a long staff with a handrest in the shape of a papyrus flower. The fertile soil of Egypt was black and in magic black was the color associated with regeneration; its use in these statues was probably meant to give them life.

The doorway leading to the Burial Chamber was blocked in a similar way to the doorways of the entrance corridor and the Antechamber. It was covered with a coating of mud plaster on which were seal impressions of Tutankhamun except at the bottom, where there were the seals of the necropolis staff, showing that the ancient robbers had also broken into that chamber. The re-filled hole would have been just large enough to admit a slender man or a boy. In this photograph it is covered by a basket and some rushes placed there by Carter. On each side of the doorway are the black wooden statues, each facing slightly inward as if looking at the door.

Three months after spying the "glint of gold" in the Antechamber, Carter was ready to dismantle the blocking of the doorway between it and the chamber beyond. On Friday, February 17, 1923, in the presence of Lord Carnarvon, Lady Evelyn Herbert, and about twenty guests, he chipped away the plaster and picked out the small stones at the top of the blocking until, after about ten minutes, he had made a large enough hole to look into the chamber. With the aid of an electric torch he could see, less than a yard away, what appeared to be a solid wall of gold. The blocking stones beneath the uppermost layers were large and roughly shaped; there was a risk of tipping them into the chamber and damaging its contents, but with the help of Arthur Mace, his assistant lent by the Metropolitan Museum (standing by the basket in the left-hand photograph), each stone was safely lifted and taken out of the tomb. The explanation of the "wall of gold" was soon forthcoming: it was the side of a large gilded shrine within which he felt confident that he would find the sarcophagus and perhaps the mummy of the king. But the robbers had been there first, and the extent of their plunder had still to be discovered.

The shrine, seventeen feet long, eleven feet wide, and nine feet high, fitted the Burial Chamber so closely that the space between it and the walls was no more than two feet and its roof almost touched the ceiling. It was the outermost of four floor-less shrines placed one above another and each with two-leaf doors at one end. They had been assembled in the chamber from some eighty sections, all of which were made of wooden planks about 2¼ inches in thickness and overlaid with gold upon a layer of plaster. In some places the bond between the plaster and the wood had become loose, owing to the shrinkage of the wood in the dry atmosphere of the tomb. Clearly the shrines had been erected before the partition wall between the two chambers had been built, and consequently before they could be dismantled the wall had to be demolished. There was very little space for using tackle to lift the individual sections, but with patience and ingenuity the problems were overcome and the whole operation was completed in eighty-four days.

Standing on the floor of the chamber, in front of the doors of the shrine, was this triple lamp (opposite), carved from a single piece of alabaster. It represents a lotus plant growing in a pond. At the head of each stem is a flower, the middlemost being fully open and those at the sides half-open. Beneath the half-open flowers are leaves, which appear to be floating on the surface of the water. The flowers held the vegetable oil in which the wicks were placed, either floating or kept upright by holders. The wicks were made of braided fibers of flax. Salt might have been put in the oil to reduce smoke.

This page: Almost identical emblems of Anubis, the jackal god of mummification, were placed at the western ends of the corridors, one on each side of the outermost shrine. Each consists of an alabaster vessel supporting an upright pole to which an imitation of a headless inflated animal skin is attached by the tail, tipped with a papyrus flower. The pole, representing a lotus stem and bud, and the skin are made of wood coated with plaster and gilded. In very remote times it was the fetish of a god named "He who is in his wrappings" (Imiut), who was later assimilated with Anubis. A much earlier example with a real animal skin stuffed and wrapped in bandages was found by the Metropolitan Museum expedition at Lisht.

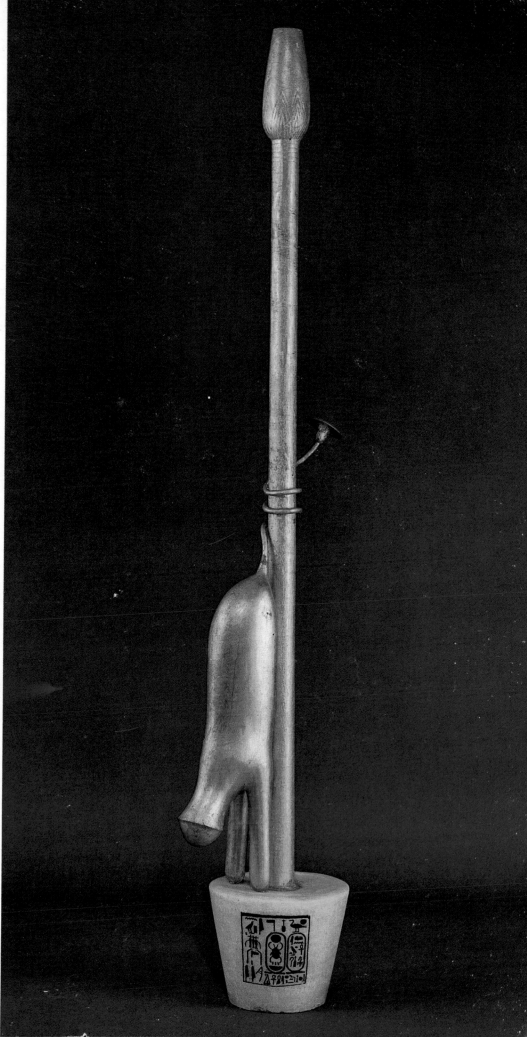

In design, this alabaster lamp, found in the corridor between the shrine and the partition wall, is without parallel. The chalice-shaped cup is flanked by figures of the god of eternity, Heh, squatting above clumps of papyrus and holding the emblems of everlasting life to the king's names. Inside the cup is a close-fitting alabaster lining, on the outer surface of which are painted figures of the king and queen and a band of inscription between floral garlands. When the floating wick was lighted, these paintings shone through the wall of the cup, but were otherwise invisible.

The second picture shows the corridor between the shrine and the north wall. On the floor are five paddles and five steering oars, for the use of the king in his afterlife. At the far end is the Anubis emblem.

Carter's difficulties were not at an end when he had dismantled the four shrines. The individual sections were taken to the field laboratory for first-aid treatment and were then packed. With other objects they were loaded on trucks which ran on an improvised track, laid progressively as the trucks advanced from the Valley to the riverbank, a distance of more than five miles. From there they were taken by steamboat four hundred miles downstream to Cairo.

This picture shows the outermost shrine as re-erected in the Cairo Museum. The outer walls are decorated with the pillar symbols of Osiris and the girdle symbols of Isis in alternate pairs, set against a background of bright blue faience inlay. On the door panel is a decapitated animal with its paws cut off, representing a mutilated foe of Osiris. The interior walls are covered with religious texts, mainly from the Book of the Dead, figures of deities, and religious symbols.

A linen pall, ornamented with gilded bronze marguerites, was supported on a light wooden framework between the outermost shrine and the second. Already decayed (but not beyond restoration) when found, and torn by the weight of the marguerites, it perished completely through neglect during a long dispute between Carter and the authorities when the tomb was closed and access to the laboratory and its environs was forbidden.

Walls and corridors of royal tombs in the Valley of the Kings are generally painted with texts and illustrations taken from religious compositions relating to the underworld. In Tutankhamun's tomb only the walls of the Burial Chamber have paintings: they are simpler and lack the underworld texts. He is here represented as the god Osiris whose resurrection he hoped to emulate.

Part of the framework of the pall can be seen on the left, and also some of the objects found in the narrow space between the first and second shrines. One of these objects was a fine alabaster unguent jar. Carved in one piece with its lid is a figure of a recumbent lion. The exterior surface is decorated with scenes of animals, mostly engaged in combat. Beneath the jar are crossbars terminating in heads of bearded Asiatics and Negroes with earrings. Its contents proved to be animal fat and resin or balsam.

Overleaf: From very early times Egyptian kings were occasionally represented as lions or sphinxes. This lion bears the name of Tutankhamun. The pose was an innovation dating from shortly before the time of Tutankhamun. Another new feature, the protruding tongue (made of ivory stained red), is also to be seen in the representations of the lion-headed god Bes above the lotus columns.

Another object found between the two outer shrines was this perfume vase, made of four pieces of alabaster cemented together. The idea conveyed by its symbolism is that the Nile will provide the king and queen, whose names are inscribed on the vase, with its contents. The vulture with the so-called **atef** crown on its head represents either Mut or Nekhbet protecting the perfume. Flanking the vase are two deities with pendulous breasts and potbellies, both named Hapi, who personify the Nile and its fertility. They are differentiated by the lily and papyrus clusters on their heads as Hapi of Upper Egypt and Hapi of Lower Egypt.

The two divisions of the country and its Nile are further symbolized by the lily and papyrus stems tied to the neck of the vase and held by the two Hapis, each of whom also supports a column representing a single stem and flower of one of the same plants, surmounted by a cobra wearing the crown of Upper or Lower Egypt. In the openwork panels of the stand beneath the vase are figures of falcons with solar disks mounted on the hieroglyphic sign for "gold," protecting with their outspread wings the cartouches inscribed with the king's names and flanked by scepters which symbolize "dominion." The piece is embellished with gold and painted ivory.

Two staffs wrapped in linen were among the other objects found between the two outermost shrines. One was made of silver and the other of gold; otherwise they were identical in appearance and each bore a chubby little figure of Tutankhamun.

These staffs are among the many objects from the tomb which remain unparalleled in Egyptian art; their use has not yet been convincingly explained. In form they recall the standards carried by priests and officials in state and religious ceremonies, but such standards are longer – these staffs are less than fifty-two inches high – and are never topped by a human figure. Perhaps they were wands or marking pegs used in some ceremony. Their short size, coupled with the childlike appearance of the figure, might suggest that the ceremony was Tutankhamun's coronation, which took place when he was only about nine years old.

Until Carter had opened the doors of the outermost shrine, there was nothing to show that the robbers had not succeeded in reaching the mummy and in stripping it of its equipment. On opening those doors, however, he could see that the seals on the doors of the second shrine were unbroken and what lay beyond must have remained untouched since the day of Tutankhamun's funeral. In the picture on the right, Carter is holding one of the doors of the second shrine and gazing at the third shrine. The whole shrine, both inside and outside, is covered with magical texts, figures of deities, and symbols connected with the underworld. As an example, the picture on the left shows part of the back wall. The female figure with outspread wings standing on the symbol for gold represents the goddess Nephthys, and the magical utterance ascribed to her is written in the inscription.

Most of the walls of Tutankhamun's shrines were covered with representations of underworld spirits and mysterious symbols, often accompanied by a kind of running commentary, written partly in the normal hieroglyphic script and partly in an enigmatic hieroglyphic script which is still largely undeciphered. Even when the individual elements in a scene are evident, their significance is usually obscure. As an example, the central feature in the left-hand picture is clearly the mummy of Tutankhamun, with serpents which bite their tails encircling his head and feet, but no meaning can be given to it. Still less is it possible to understand the scene on the right with its fire-spitting serpents, mummiform figures, and pairs of arms supporting disks, two rising from the earth and two descending from the sky.

The sister goddesses, Isis and Nephthys, are represented on the inner face of the doors of the third shrine, with wings outspread symbolizing their function as protectors of Tutankhamun's mummy. Each goddess utters a magical spell, which is inscribed in the spaces around their bodies; they promise the king everlasting life, accompanying the sun god Ra in his boat across the sky by day and through the underworld at night. On the lintel above the door is the winged disk with pendent cobras, symbolizing the god named Horus of Behdet.

In the Valley of the Kings the tombs were guarded by officials who put their seal on the doors. In Tutankhamun's tomb they also sealed the doors of the inner shrines. The motif on the necropolis seal, shown above, was a recumbent jackal over nine bound captives.

242

Tutankhamun's shrines diminished rather irregularly in size, so that the width of the corridors between them varied from about four feet to about eighteen inches. Some of the objects placed in the corridors of the outermost shrine and the second—the widest—and of the second and the third have already been described. Between the third and fourth shrines the objects found included two remarkable ostrich-feather fans, one made of ebony overlaid with gold and encrusted with semiprecious stones and the other of wood overlaid with gold. The alternate white and brown feathers—thirty in each fan—had been almost entirely destroyed by insects, but it was the decoration of their palms which made them outstanding, and particularly the decoration of the gold fan, shown in detail on the next pages. Similar fans are frequently shown on monuments being carried behind kings, and at the present day their modern counterparts are borne behind the pope when he is seated on the sedia gestatoria.

An inscription on the handle of the fan states that it is made of "ostrich feathers obtained by His Majesty when hunting in the desert east of Heliopolis." Incidents in the hunt are depicted on both sides of the palm (overleaf). On this side Tutankhamun is represented riding in a chariot and drawing a bow. In order that his hands may be free, he has put the reins around his body. Two wounded ostriches are about to be dispatched by the king's hound. Behind the king is a short inscription which reads: "May all protection of life attend him"–a wish symbolized by the life sign with human arms and legs following the chariot and carrying an approximate replica of this fan.

Pages 112-113: On this side of the palm Tutankhamun is shown returning from the hunt. The spirited horses are held in check, the reins being now in the king's hands, together with his bow and whip. Instead of a leopard-skin corselet, worn during the hunt, he has put on a pleated garment and a shoulder wrap with feathered fringes. Two attendants carry the dead ostriches on their shoulders. Since a fully-grown ostrich of the species Struthio Camelus, which survived in Egypt until about 150 years ago, would weigh approximately 345 pounds, this detail, at least, is a flight of imagination. The inscription above the scene compares the king's skill at shooting with that of the goddess Bastet and the strength of his horses with that of bulls.

The folding doors of Tutankhamun's shrines were fastened by ebony bolts which slid sideways through silver staples at the top and bottom of each pair of doors. In the middle were two more staples, one on each door, through which a long piece of rope was first threaded backward and forward horizontally three or four times and then wound round the horizontal strands and tied. Finally a lump of mud was placed on the knot and sealed. Two scarab-shaped seals were used, one the official seal of the necropolis staff engraved with a recumbent jackal over nine captives and the other identical but with Tutankhamun's name added. The captives represented Egypt's traditional enemies and the jackal the god Anubis, who was primarily in charge of mummification but on the seals he seems to be protecting the necropolis against all invaders. The doors of the innermost shrine with their bolts drawn and sealed rope removed are shown in the right-hand picture. Inside the doors can be seen one end of the king's stone sarcophagus.

The box of this fine sarcophagus is made of brown quartzite and the lid is made of pink granite tinted to the color of the box. Why two different stones should have been used is not obvious, unless the reason was that the intended quartzite lid was not ready in time for the funeral and a granite lid of indifferent quality, which happened to be available, was substituted for it. There was another puzzle too: the granite lid was broken in two and the fracture, which was concealed with cement and paint, must have occurred before the shrines were put in position. No explanation seems possible, except that the king's premature death made it necessary to hurry the work and an accident happened.

Symbolism for magical purposes was an important feature of Egyptian funerary equipment. On the sarcophagus it is seen most clearly in the graceful figures of four goddesses, Isis, Nephthys, Neith, and Selket, carved in high relief on the corners, their wings outspread to protect the body within the sarcophagus.

When the lid of the sarcophagus was raised and a linen shroud removed, it was not Tutankhamun's mummy which could be seen, but the outermost of three coffins fitting one inside another, all in the human form of the god Osiris. This coffin was made of wood overlaid with thin gold on a layer of plaster. Osiris's emblems, the crook and the flail encrusted with gold, faience, and colored glass, were in his hands and a small wreath of flowers was tied around the vulture and the cobra on his headdress. The features were those of Tutankhamun and, by giving him the outward form of Osiris, who had risen from the dead through the magic powers of his wife Isis, it was believed that his survival would be ensured.

One of the most pleasing little objects found in the Burial Chamber was this gold perfume box, which consists of two cartouche-shaped compartments mounted on a silver pedestal. Usually cartouches contain the names of the king, but in this box they enclose images of him wearing the side lock of a child. His face in one image is black, perhaps for magical reasons.

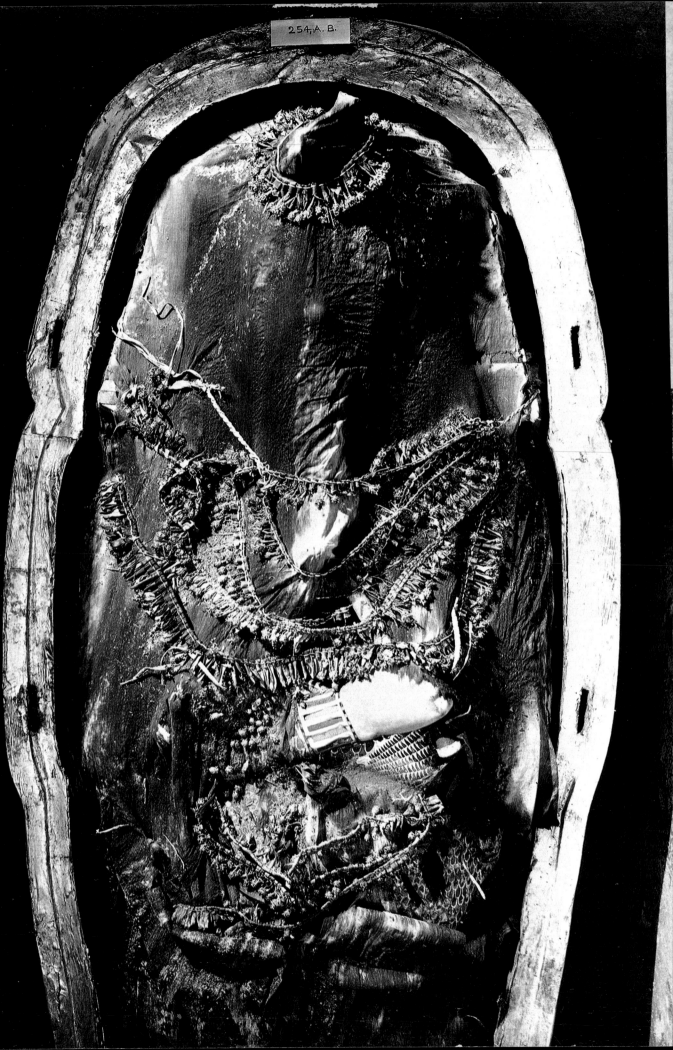

Another linen shroud lay over the middle coffin. This time the wreath around the vulture and cobra was outside the shroud, together with a floral garland lower on the body. Both contained olive leaves, blue lotus petals, and cornflowers fastened to strips of papyrus, but in the garland there were also leaves of willow and wild celery. In the picture below Carter is shown removing the shroud. The picture on the left shows what he saw. The whole coffin is made of wood overlaid with sheet gold on a coating of plaster and inlaid with colored glass in imitation of red jasper, lapis lazuli, and turquoise and set in a feather pattern. Over the upper part of the body are representations of a cobra and a vulture, protecting the king with their outspread wings.

The lids of this coffin and the outermost were fastened to the boxes by silver tongues, which fitted into slots cut downward from the tops of the walls of the boxes. Gold-headed silver pins, driven horizontally through the walls and the tongues, kept the lids securely fixed.

Between the sarcophagus and the outermost coffin there was just enough space to pull out the silver pins and thus release the lid, but the middle coffin fitted the outermost so closely that the pins could only be extracted about a quarter of an inch. They were eventually removed by, first, lifting the whole nest of coffins until it rested on planks laid across the top of the sarcophagus. Strong wires were then fixed to timbers vertically above the coffin and attached to the projecting ends of the pins. The outermost coffin was finally lowered by ropes and pulleys to the floor of the sarcophagus, leaving the middle coffin suspended on the wires.

In this picture the middle coffin is resting on planks laid across the top of the sarcophagus; the box of the outermost coffin is beneath the planks inside the sarcophagus. The tackle on which the middle coffin was suspended has been dismantled; the silver pins can now be extracted without difficulty and the lid lifted.

Something which perplexed Carter was the great weight of the coffins; they were far heavier than the thickness of the wood seemed to explain. At least until the lid of this coffin had been removed the cause of this unexpected heaviness remained a mystery.

It is hard to imagine the amount of work which must have been
put into making this coffin. Carved in wood, it was first overlaid
with sheet gold on a thin layer of plaster. Narrow strips of gold,
placed on edge, were then soldered to the base to form cells in
which small pieces of colored glass, fixed with cement, were
laid. The technique is known as Egyptian cloisonné work, but it
is not true cloisonné because the glass was already shaped
before being put in the cells (cloisons), and not put in the cells
in powder form and fused by heating.

As soon as the lid of the middle coffin was raised, the reason for the immense weight of the nest of coffins became apparent. The innermost coffin was made of solid gold. It was over six feet in length and about one-eighth of an inch in thickness. When weighed it turned the scale at 296 pounds troy (110.4 kilograms). A large amount of fatty resinous perfume had been poured over the coffin, so much that it filled most of the space between the gold coffin and the middle coffin.

Like the wooden coffins, this coffin was covered with a linen shroud upon which had been placed an elaborate collar composed of leaves, flowers, berries, and fruits together with blue glass beads, all attached to a semicircular sheet of papyrus. Also like the wooden coffins, it represents Tutankhamun as the god Osiris holding his regular emblems, the crook and flail; the features are those of the king himself. On the neck is a two-string necklace of gold and blue faience beads. Necklaces of this kind were awarded by Egyptian kings to military commanders and high officials for distinguished services. A broad bead collar spans the chest and on the wrists are bracelets encrusted with similar, but smaller, beads. Superimposed in cloisonné work over the arms and abdomen are figures of the vulture of Nekhbet and the cobra of Wadjet (with the body of a vulture), goddesses of Upper and Lower Egypt, each of them grasping in her talons the hieroglyphic sign for "infinity." On the lower part of the coffin are engraved figures of Isis and Nephthys with outspread wings.

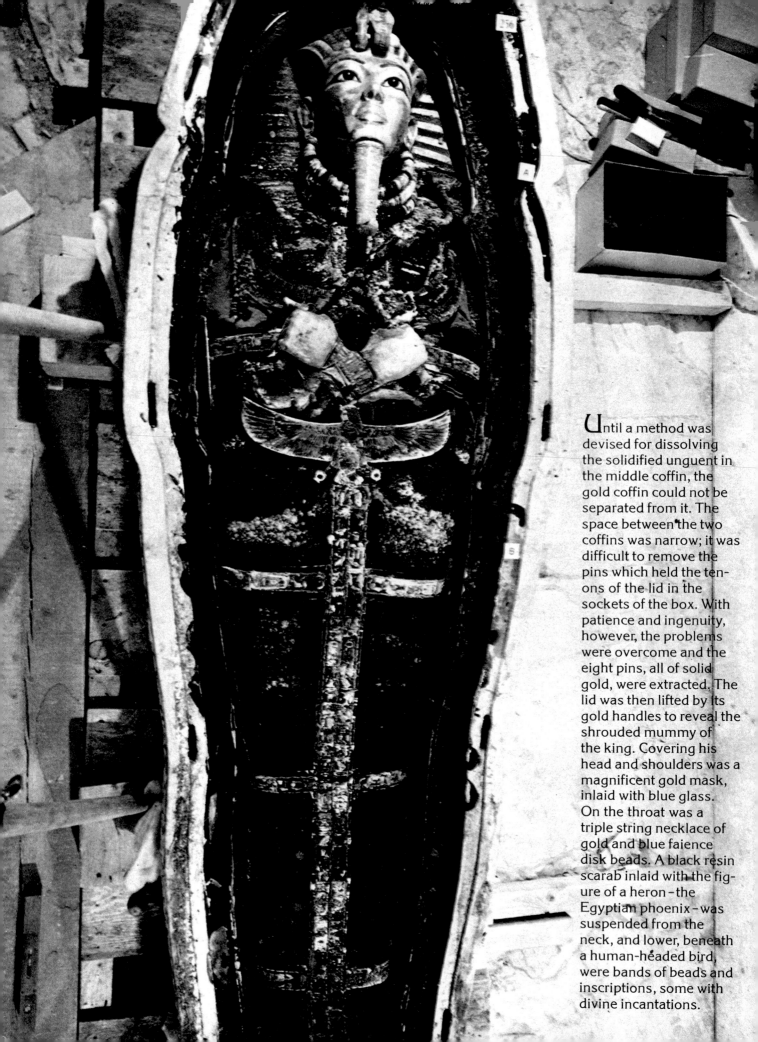

Until a method was devised for dissolving the solidified unguent in the middle coffin, the gold coffin could not be separated from it. The space between the two coffins was narrow; it was difficult to remove the pins which held the tenons of the lid in the sockets of the box. With patience and ingenuity, however, the problems were overcome and the eight pins, all of solid gold, were extracted. The lid was then lifted by its gold handles to reveal the shrouded mummy of the king. Covering his head and shoulders was a magnificent gold mask, inlaid with blue glass. On the throat was a triple string necklace of gold and blue faience disk beads. A black resin scarab inlaid with the figure of a heron – the Egyptian phoenix – was suspended from the neck, and lower, beneath a human-headed bird, were bands of beads and inscriptions, some with divine incantations.

Tutankhamun's coffins and his mummy were
made in the traditional form of the god Osiris, so
that, through imitative magic, his body would
be reanimated just as the dead body of Osiris had
been revivified. As a deceased king, however, he
had another chance of survival: by being identified
with the sun god, whose body was made of
gold and his hair of lapis lazuli. This mask with its
gold face and neck, and its eyebrows and
eyelashes of lapis lazuli, seems to represent him as
the sun god and thereby to secure for him
a solar afterlife.

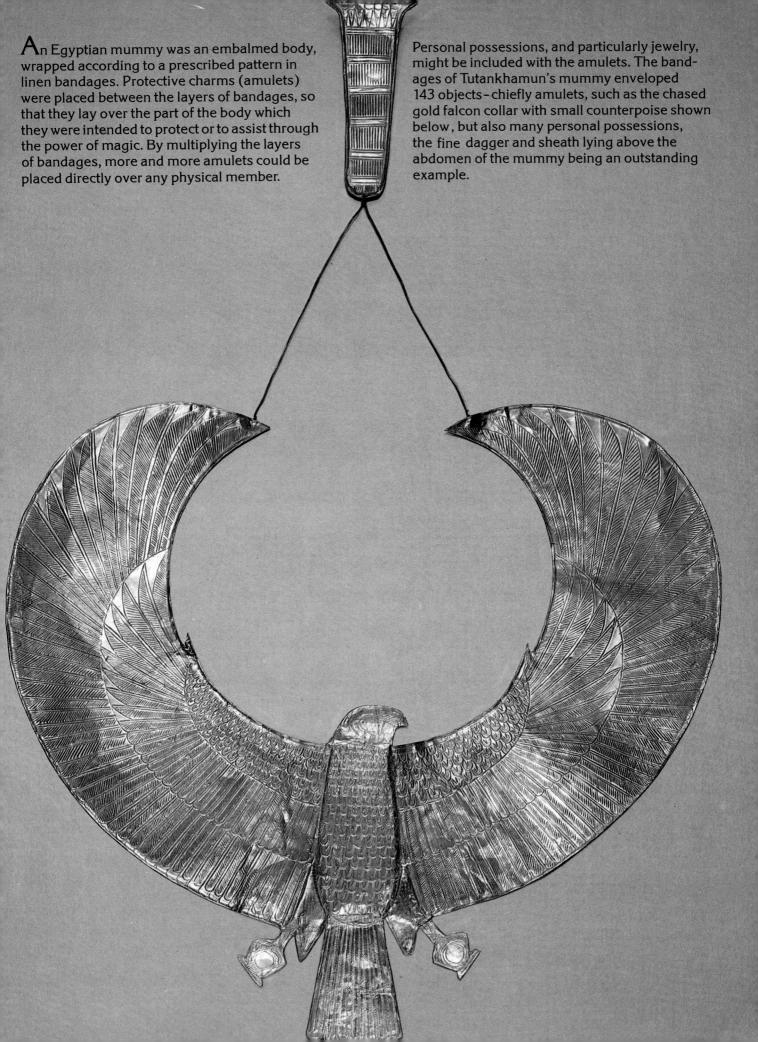

An Egyptian mummy was an embalmed body, wrapped according to a prescribed pattern in linen bandages. Protective charms (amulets) were placed between the layers of bandages, so that they lay over the part of the body which they were intended to protect or to assist through the power of magic. By multiplying the layers of bandages, more and more amulets could be placed directly over any physical member.

Personal possessions, and particularly jewelry, might be included with the amulets. The bandages of Tutankhamun's mummy enveloped 143 objects – chiefly amulets, such as the chased gold falcon collar with small counterpoise shown below, but also many personal possessions, the fine dagger and sheath lying above the abdomen of the mummy being an outstanding example.

There can be little doubt that this dagger was a treasured possession. Engraved on its blade of hardened gold is a design consisting of a diamond-pattern frieze and a palmette with poppies above two perpendicular incisions which resemble floral stems. The handle is largely decorated with alternate bands of geometric patterns in very fine granulated goldwork and lily-palmette designs in cloisonné work of semiprecious stones and glass. One side of the sheath is ornamented with a feather inlay between a palmette frieze and a jackal's head at the point. The other side is embossed with ibexes, a calf, and a bull being attacked by lions, hounds, and a leopard, and lastly a fleeing calf. An elaborate floral device fills the base.

Even in prehistoric times (before about 3100 B.C.) iron obtained from meteorites was used in Egypt, no doubt infrequently, for making beads. Nevertheless very few examples dating from before the time of Tutankhamun have yet been discovered. The iron blade of this dagger and a few other objects of iron, all small, found in his tomb may have been made of metal received as a gift from one of the kings of western Asia, perhaps the king of the Hittites, who were accomplished in the techniques of ironworking. The decoration of the handle is very similar to that of the gold dagger, but the pommel is different. Whereas in the gold dagger the pommel bore the king's names in embossed sheet gold, the pommel of this dagger, made of rock crystal, is uninscribed. The sheath is made of gold.

Painted representations of amulets on coffins dating from about five hundred years before the time of Tutankhamun include groups of five cobras and five vultures placed near the deceased person's head. Five gold vultures were found in the neck bandages of Tutankhamun's mummy grouped with three, or possibly four, cobras (one human-headed with wings). This cobra was found in a different layer of bandages, but also over the neck. Egyptian embalmers were sometimes careless in arranging amulets and it is possible that this cobra was simply misplaced. Alternatively, it may have been intended as an independent amulet, the purpose of which is not known. It is made of sheet gold, embossed and chased. A cobra in repose, which it represents, was used as the hieroglyphic sign for the sound **dj,** but it has no such significance in this instance.

Seventeen collars were placed in the bandages of Tutankhamun's mummy. Some of them were composed of beads, but the majority were made of gold, either plain with the details chased or inlaid with semiprecious stones or colored glass in cloisonné work. As an example of the technical skill of the Egyptian jeweler, this collar is one of the finest. It represents the vulture of the Upper Egyptian goddess Nekhbet, and it was placed over the chest of the mummy, the tips of the wings reaching the shoulders. A floral counterpoise, which was attached by gold wires to eyelets at the back of the wings, hung down the back of the mummy. The wings consist of 250 gold segments, chased on the back and inlaid on the front with "feathers" of polychrome glass in imitation of turquoise, jasper, and lapis lazuli. Adjacent segments are held together by thread passed through small gold eyelets which project from the upper and lower edges. Both the beak and the eye are made of obsidian. In each talon the bird grasps the hieroglyphic sign for "infinity" (**shen**), inlaid with red and blue glass.

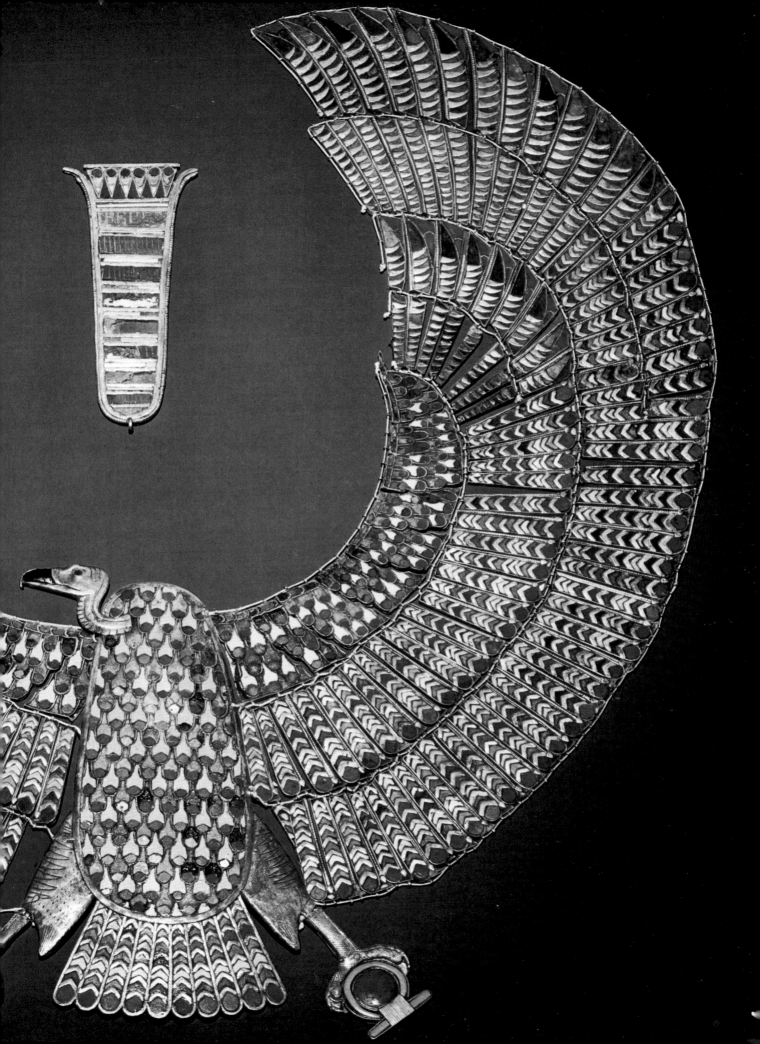

Thirteen bracelets were placed on the forearms and wrists of Tutankhamun's mummy, seven on the right and six on the left, and a further eleven were distributed elsewhere between the layers of wrappings. Some were merely ornamental and others embodied amuletic devices. These two bracelets were among the thirteen found on the body and both belong to the ornamental class. Set in the bracelet on the left is a jewel which is believed to be turquoise, and its wrist strap is made of tubes representing the bound stems of the papyrus and lily flowers at the hinge and the clasp. The jewel in the right-hand bracelet is lapis lazuli. Both jewels are surrounded by applied granular work, small bosses, bands of braided rope, and continuous spirals.

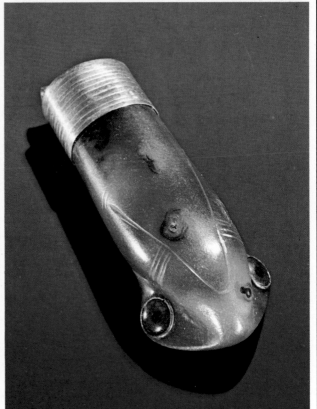

Of the fifteen rings found on Tutankhamun's mummy, only two were placed on his fingers. The uppermost in this group, incised with figures of the king and the god Min, is made, probably, of nephrite, and the lowest of chalcedony. The bezel of the middle ring consists of three-dimensional figures of a falcon, a lapis lazuli scarab, and the bark of the moon.

Made of carnelian and suspended on a gold wire, this amulet lay on the left side of the mummy's throat. Its name was Menqebit (sometimes written Menqerit), which suggests something cool (**menqeb** was a word for "fan" and the amulet was to ensure cool refreshment for the throat). The painted eyes are overlaid with clear quartz and outlined with gold.

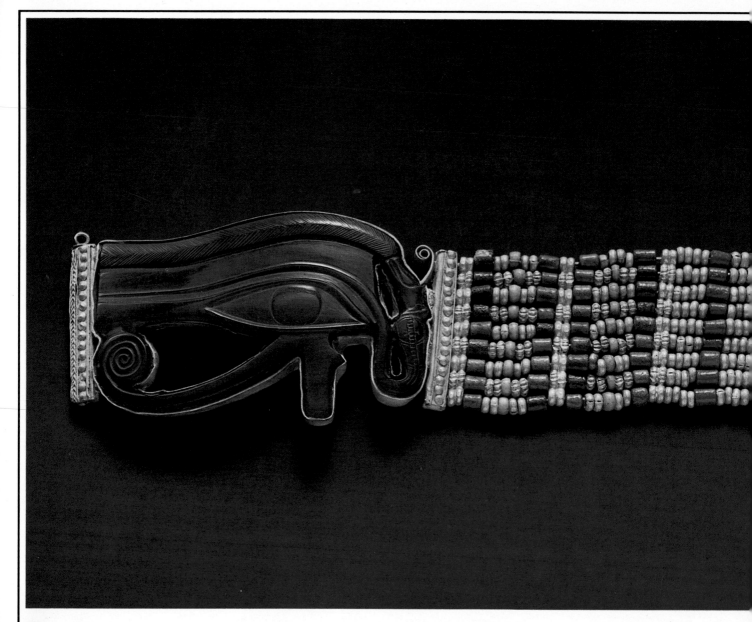

The central feature of this bracelet (above), found on the mummy's right arm, represents a human eye, combined with the markings of a falcon's head. It was called **udjat,** a word which means "sound, healthy." According to legend, Horus lost an eye fighting with the god Seth to avenge the murder of his father, Osiris. Thoth, the god of magic, found the eye and healed it– hence the name. Horus, however, gave it to the dead Osiris to eat, thereby restoring him to life. Carved in one piece of carnelian with the **udjat** is a cobra wearing the double crown of Upper and Lower Egypt.

The second from the top of these rings (opposite) was found on the middle finger of Tutankhamun's left hand. On its bezel is a figure of the king kneeling and holding in his outstretched hands an image of the goddess Maat. On the bezels of the other rings, from top to bottom, are the following motifs: Tutankhamun presenting an offering to Ra-Harakhty; the god Amen-Ra; the king's throne name and his original name, Tutankhaton; the god Ra-Harakhty.

Overleaf: Made of solid gold, the pendant of this necklace represents the vulture of Nekhbet, with the ends of the wings folded like a cloak. It is encrusted with polychrome glass, which fits the cells so perfectly that it has been regarded as a rare example of true cloisonné work. The clasp consists of two falcons with their heads turned backward; a gold tenon on the inner side of one bird slides into a gold mortise on the inner side of the other bird. It was found in the eleventh or twelfth layer of bandages.

Pages 150–151: As a work of art, the reverse of this pendant is hardly inferior to the outer face, though technically very different. The whole surface is minutely chased in imitation of the vulture's feathers. Undoubtedly the most striking feature is the head, with its wrinkled occiput, obsidian eyes, and lapis lazuli beak. Modeled in relief, so as to appear to be suspended from the vulture's neck, are a miniature necklace and pendant. The pendant consists of a cartouche inscribed with the king's name, flanked by two cobras and surmounted by two ostrich plumes with the sun's disk. Probably this necklace was worn by the king in his lifetime.

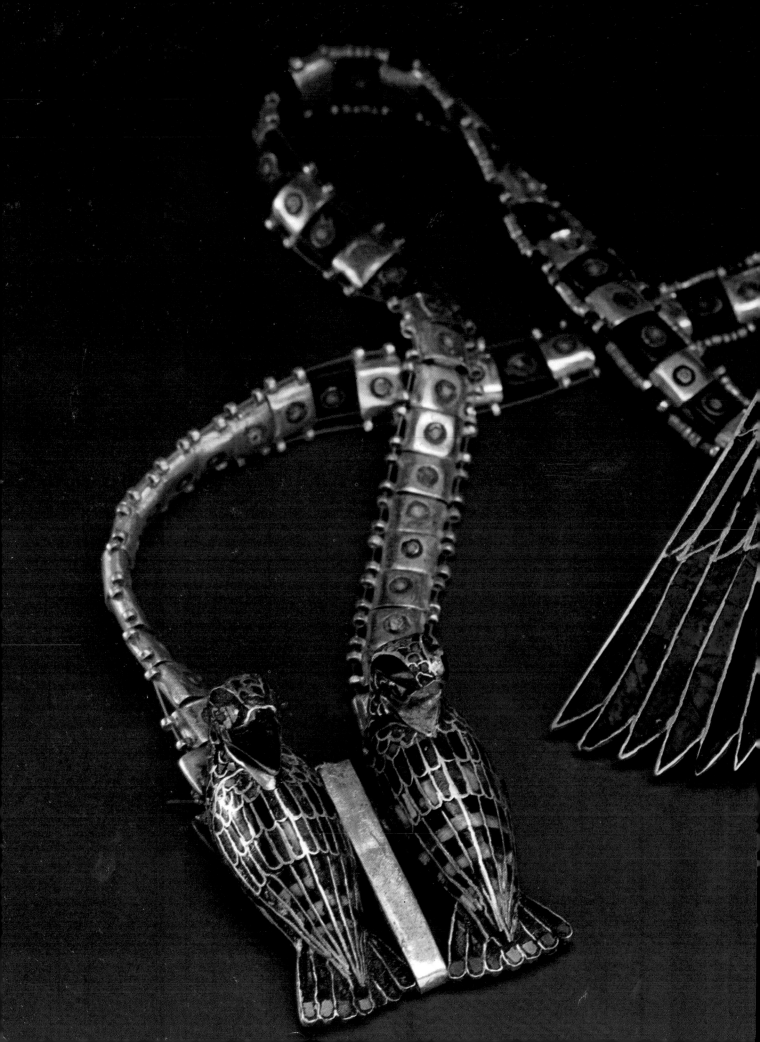

Placed like a sentinel at the entrance to the so-called Treasury was a lifelike figure of a recumbent jackal upon a shrine which contained several pieces of jewelry. It was carved of wood, overlaid with a thin layer of plaster and painted with black resin; the wooden shrine was gilded. The body of the jackal was almost completely covered with linen draperies, one of which proved to be a shirt dated in the seventh year of Akhenaton's reign, about the time of Tutankhamun's birth. Beneath the shrine was a sledge with carrying poles.

As a hieroglyphic sign, a recumbent jackal upon a shrine signifies both the jackal god Anubis and the title "He who is over the secrets." This figure may have been intended to combine Anubis's role as a guard with his being a custodian of secret things.

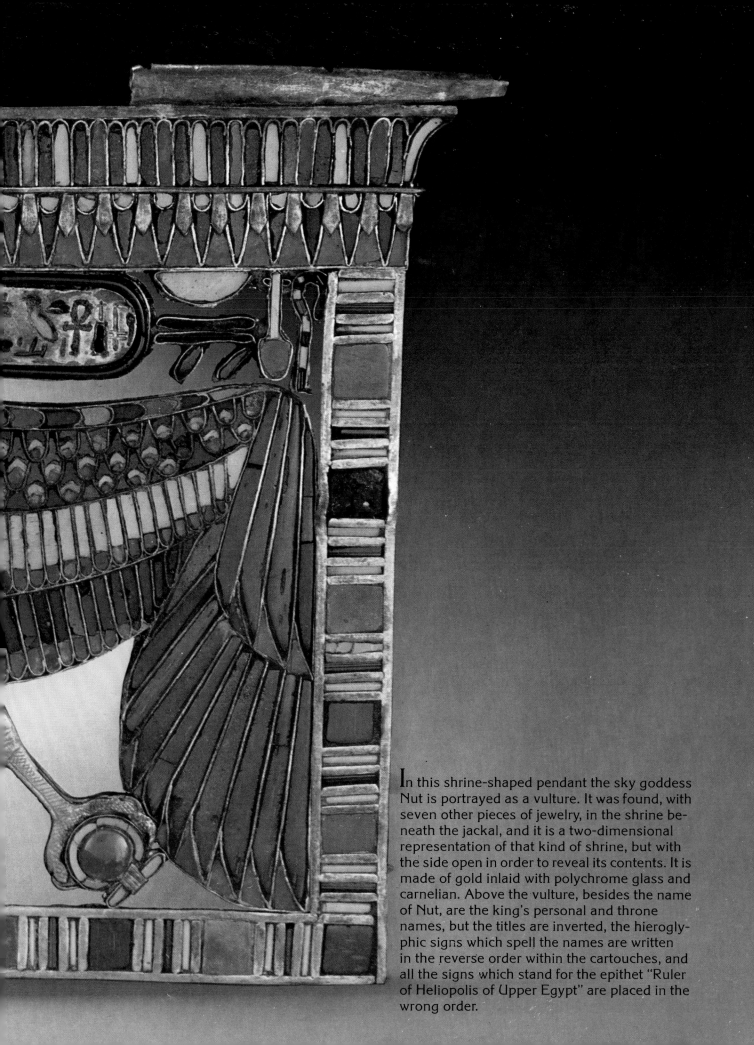

In this shrine-shaped pendant the sky goddess Nut is portrayed as a vulture. It was found, with seven other pieces of jewelry, in the shrine beneath the jackal, and it is a two-dimensional representation of that kind of shrine, but with the side open in order to reveal its contents. It is made of gold inlaid with polychrome glass and carnelian. Above the vulture, besides the name of Nut, are the king's personal and throne names, but the titles are inverted, the hieroglyphic signs which spell the names are written in the reverse order within the cartouches, and all the signs which stand for the epithet "Ruler of Heliopolis of Upper Egypt" are placed in the wrong order.

Nut is again represented on the pendant at the left, not, however, as a vulture but as a woman with vulture's wings. In the inscription beneath the wings, she declares that she has spread her wings over Tutankhamun and has given him her protection. Both this pendant and the one shown below were found in the shrine-shaped pedestal of the jackal figure.

The central feature of the pendant below is a winged scarab, which pushes the names of Tutankhamun instead of, as more usually, the sun's disk at its rebirth each morning. On the back of the scarab, however, is engraved a text from the Book of the Dead instructing Tutankhamun's heart not to give evidence against the king at his last judgment — an entirely different function of the scarab; such scarabs were usually placed over the heart (the supposed seat of intelligence) in the wrappings of mummies. Isis and Nephthys support the scarab's wings and recite incantations to the sun god. The winged sun's disk at the top represents Horus of Behdet flying the reborn sun across the sky.

Hathor, as goddess of the Theban necropolis, was often shown as a cow emerging from a papyrus swamp, only her head being visible. The gilded wooden cow's head at the right appears to represent Hathor in that role

When mummifying a body Egyptian embalmers removed the lungs, liver, intestines, and stomach, and embalmed them separately. The mummified organs were then put in four jars, called in modern times Canopic jars, and the jars put in a box with four compartments for burial with the body. Tutankhamun's Canopic equipment, however, was more elaborate. The outermost protection was provided by this massive gilded wooden shrine, mounted on a sledge. Each side was guarded by one of four goddesses, Isis, Nephthys, Neith, or Selket, the last of whom is shown at right.

All four goddesses around the shrine were alike in appearance except for their emblems. They were made of gilded wood, their eyes and eyebrows painted in black. Owing to carelessness, Selket and Nephthys were transposed when the shrine was erected. Selket, illustrated here, was a scorpion goddess, as the emblem on her head indicates, and one of her special functions was the healing of scorpion stings by magic. She was also a goddess of magic in general, as well as of childbirth. In this representation she wears a pleated shawl over a close-fitting dress with short sleeves, and over both garments a broad collar modeled to imitate rows of beads. On her head is a linen kerchief into which her hair is gathered and tied at the neck. Artistically, the most unusual feature is the turn of the head, which violates the Egyptian convention that a freestanding figure must face the viewer directly. Amarna influences are displayed in the long neck and the naturalistic pose.

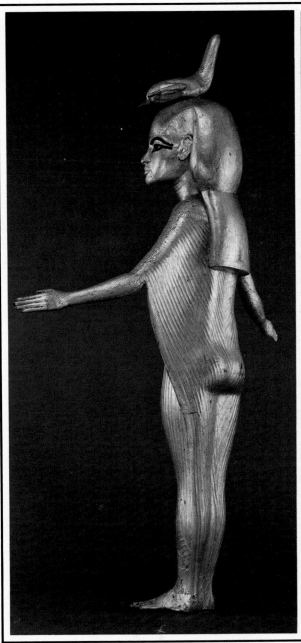
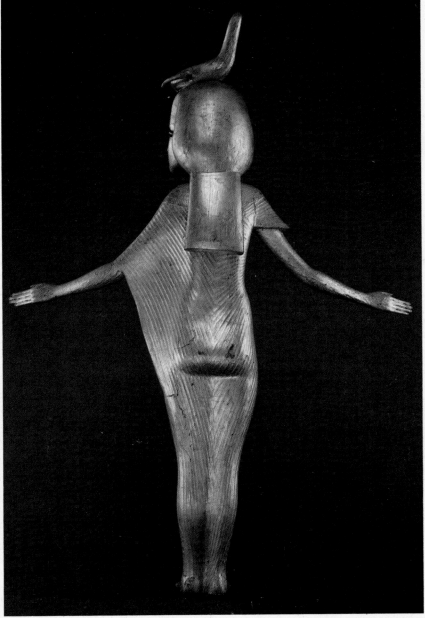

Inside the Canopic shrine was a magnificent alabaster chest with gilded dado, placed on a gilded wooden sledge and covered by a linen pall. The detachable roof, which served as the lid of the chest, was fastened by cords to gold staples near the top of the walls. At each corner was a figure, carved in high relief, representing one of the four goddesses who guarded the the outer shrine. In front of the goddesses were short inscriptions, one of which is the following: "Words spoken by Isis: 'My arms hide what is in me, I protect Imsety who is within me, [the] Imsety of the Osiris, king Nebkheperura [i.e. Tutankhamun], true of voice'." Four cavities were hewn in the interior of the chest to hold the internal organs and on top of each cavity was an alabaster stopper, a finely sculptured likeness of the king. The features were picked out in black and red and the vulture's head and cobra on the brow were inserted.

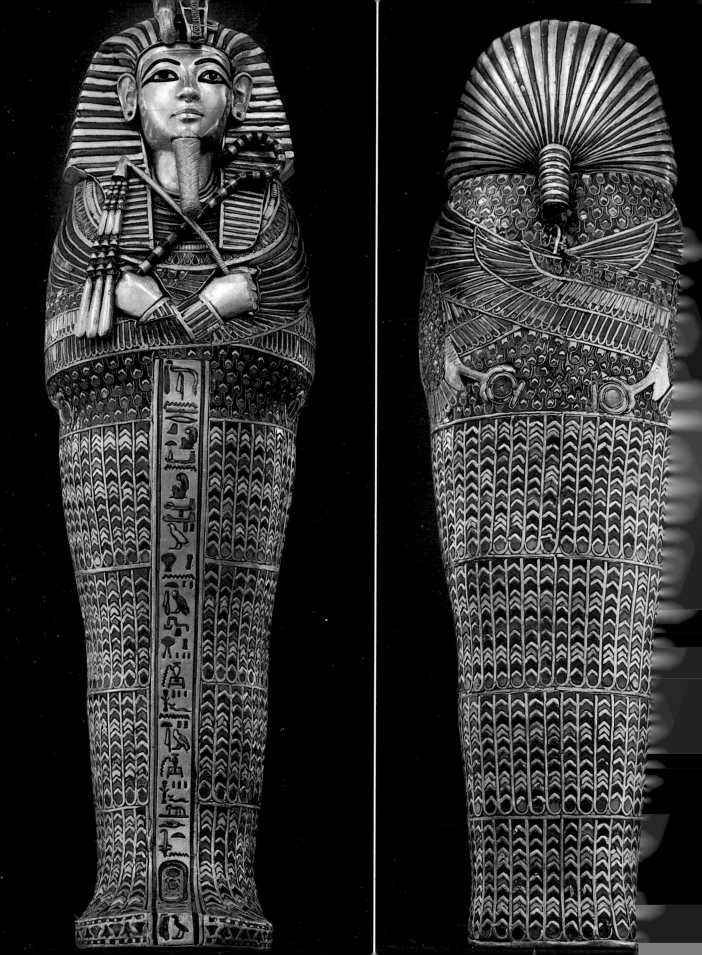

Tutankhamun's internal organs were not placed directly in the cavities of the Canopic chest but in four small coffins of solid gold inlaid with colored glass and carnelian, which were miniature replicas of his middle coffin. Each coffin represents the king as the god Osiris, wearing an artificial beard and holding the crook and flail.

The embalmed internal organs were identified with four minor deities known as the Four Sons of Horus and named Imsety (liver), Hapi (lungs), Duamutef (stomach), and Qebehsenuef (intestines), and the four goddesses, Isis, Nephthys, Neith, and Selket were the protectors of the Four Sons of Horus. Selket protected Qebehsenuef, as the inscription on the front of this coffin makes clear. It reads: "Words spoken by Selket: 'I place my arms on that which is in me, I protect Qebehsenuef who is in me, [the] Qebehsenuef of the Osiris, king Neb-kheperura [i.e. Tutankhamun], true of voice.'"

Tutankhamun's names in the inscriptions (most clearly inside the coffins) appear to have been substituted for others which have been completely erased. Like some other objects in the tomb, these coffins may have been made originally for Smenkh-kara, Akhenaton's co-regent at the end of his reign (and probably Tutankhamun's brother or half-brother).

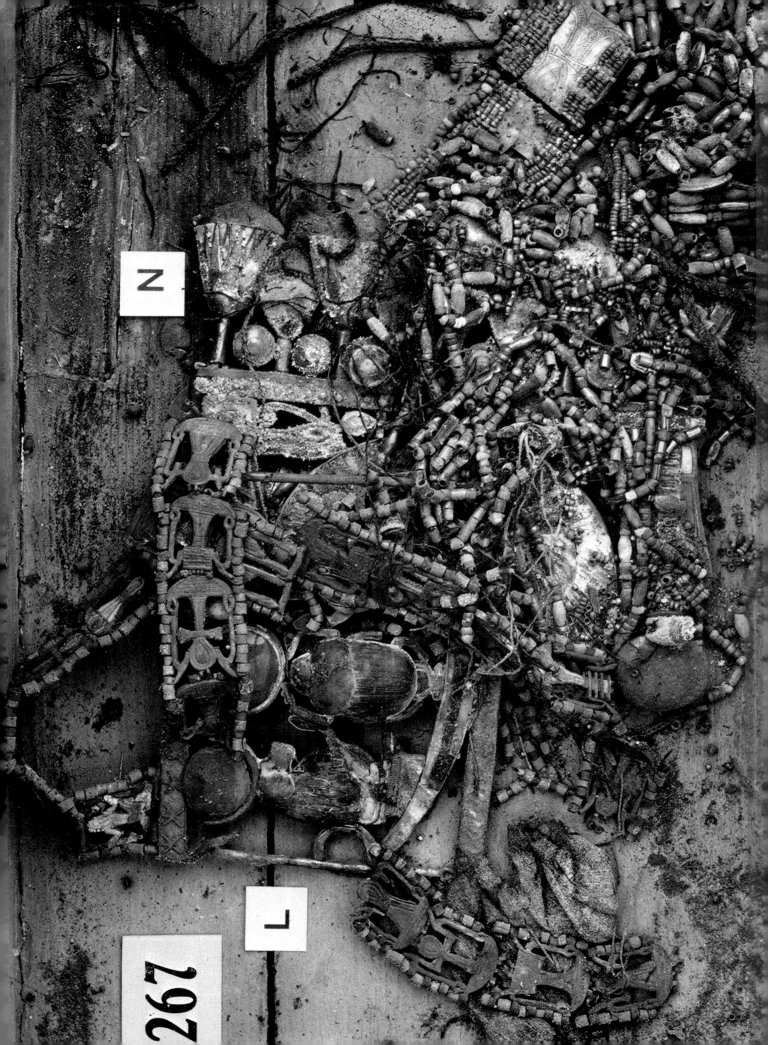

Dismantling Tutankhamun's shrines and opening his coffins involved engineering difficulties which were overcome by imagination and resourcefulness. Unpacking some of the boxes posed problems which were just as complex, though of a different kind. One box alone required three weeks' work to unpack. Probably they were tightly filled in the first instance, and the ancient thieves, in their haste, distributed the contents in a jumble on the floor, taking what seemed most valuable. The necropolis staff, apparently with equal haste, refilled the boxes with whatever came to hand, regardless of whether or not they were putting it back in its original box. Through rough handling several objects had suffered damage and in some cases parts of the same object were put in different boxes.

This box provides a good example of the state of confusion in which several of the most elaborate pieces of jewelry were found. Some of the best pieces, as they appeared after restoration, are shown in the illustrations which follow. The design of the box and its vaulted lid represents a well-known type, but what is remarkable is the ivory and ebony marquetry inlay, in which more than 45,000 pieces are set.

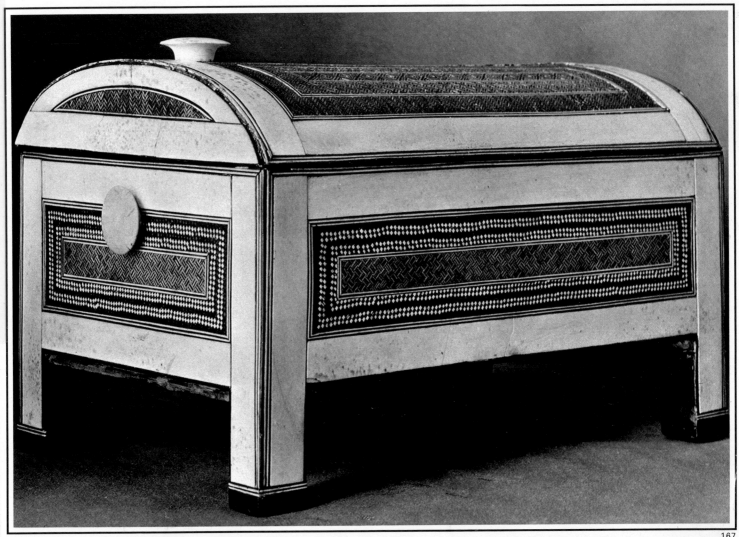

The sun god is depicted on this gold inlaid pendant (opposite) as a scarab pushing the sun's disk over the eastern horizon. He has changed from the night bark, in which he had sailed through the underworld, to his day bark, for his voyage across the celestial ocean, represented in lapis lazuli under the bark. The bark also bears two cobras with sun's disks, one in the prow and one in the stern; their tails are replaced by three amulets symbolizing stability, life, and goodness. The cobras flanking the sun have life signs on their hoods to show that the sun is bringing life to Upper and Lower Egypt.

This page: A young Egyptian is shown wearing the necklace and pendant illustrated in the previous photograph. The straps consist of separate inlaid plaques held together by rows of small beads at the sides and back. At the top of each strap is a curved shoulder piece representing the flying vulture of Nekhbet. Two strings of beads join the vultures to a clasp composed of a pair of gold cobras connected by a slide fastening.

The theme of this pendant is again the sun god in the divine bark at sunrise. It differs, however, from the pendant last illustrated in the auxiliary elements of its symbolism. The scarab, which holds the sign of "infinity" in its back claws, is flanked by two baboons squatting on gold shrines. According to Egyptian mythology, the rising sun was greeted by pairs of baboons, a concept which may have been suggested by the habit of baboons in nature of emitting shrieks at dawn. The lunar disks and crescents on the heads of these baboons seem incongruous in this context (although regular when a baboon symbolizes the moon god, Thoth). Perhaps they were added, like the two scepters signifying "dominion" at the sides, to strengthen the openwork components of the pendant. At the top is the hieroglyphic sign for the sky, inlaid with lapis lazuli and gold stars.

Two of the five names borne by Egyptian kings, as well as the names of other members of the royal family, were written in oval rings, which early scholars called cartouches, a French word meaning an ornamental tablet for an inscription. In origin, it represented a length of rope formed into a loop by tying together the two ends; it was merely an oval variant of the circular sign for "infinity" or "universality." This box, which bears Tutankhamun's name on the lid, resembles in outline a cartouche, but for practical reasons it is greater in depth. It was found on the floor of the Treasury, next to the box inlaid with ivory and ebony described earlier, and its disordered contents were likewise chiefly articles of jewelry, some of which are shown on the right. Several pieces showed signs of having been worn.

Wooden mirror case in the form of the hieroglyphic sign for "life," **ankh.** One of the Egyptian words for "mirror" was also **ankh.**

Gold cloisonné earrings representing birds with ducks' heads and falcons' wings. On the outer cap of each fastening is a portrait of the king.

Necklace with gold pendant symbolizing the moon sailing across the sky. Lotus flowers grow in the celestial waters and raindrops fall to earth.

Gold bangle with openwork scarab encrusted with lapis lazuli. At the hinge and the clasp are a mandrake fruit, poppies and marguerites.

The stiles and rails of this wooden box are veneered with ivory and its panels are ornamented with gilded hieroglyphic symbols fretted in groups of four, each group consisting of the sign for "life" between a pair of "dominion" signs standing on the sign for "all." The hieroglyphic inscriptions repeat several times Tutankhamun's five names and titles and add some common epithets. Queen Ankhesenamun is mentioned twice on the front, followed by the wish that she may "live for ever." All four feet are capped with silver. The interior is divided into sixteen compartments of uniform size which seem to have been intended for vessels, perhaps of gold or silver, though none remained in the box when it was found. The diverse objects put in the box by the necropolis staff after the robbery, two of which are illustrated on the next page, were certainly not part of its original contents.

Opposite: Egyptian scribes wrote with brushes, not pens. The brushes were made of short, slender stems of rushes, the tips of which were cut at a slant, like a chisel, and then chewed by the scribe to separate the individual fibers. In Tutankhamun's time the brushes were generally kept in a slot in a palette made of a strip of wood or ivory with two cavities at one end for solidified red and black ink. Before the invention of such composite palettes, scribes kept their brushes in tubular cases, usually hollow reeds. In this brush holder, made of wood overlaid with gold foil and inlaid with semiprecious stones and glass, the simple reed has developed into a model of a palm-tree column.

This page: From early times documents in ink were written on papyrus, the name of the material from which our word "paper" is derived. It was made in sheets from the pith of the papyrus rush, cut in long, thin slices laid side by side in two layers, one layer with the slices laid horizontally and the other vertically; the two layers were then beaten until they became matted together. When dry, the sheets were rubbed with a wooden burnisher to make the surface smooth. Tutankhamun's fragile burnisher, which is probably a model for funerary purposes, consists of two pieces of ivory; the upper part is capped with gold foil and the handle represents a stylized lily and its stem.

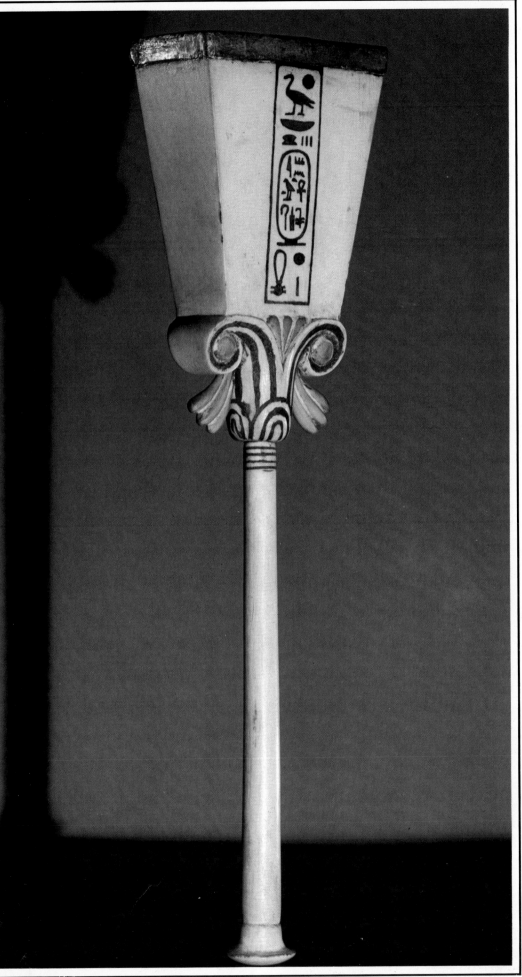

This solid gold squatting figure
and its necklace were found,
wrapped in a piece of linen,
within a gilded miniature coffin
which contained two smaller
coffins, one inside the other. The
innermost coffin bore the name
of Queen Teye, wife of one of
Tutankhamun's predecessors,
Amenhotpe III, and enclosed a
lock of her auburn hair. It has
therefore been supposed that the
figure represents Amenhotpe III,
but his name is not written on
any of the coffins, whereas the
name of Tutankhamun is inscribed on the outermost wooden
coffin and on the coffin which
contained this figure. In view of
this evidence, it seems probable
that the king represented is
Tutankhamun himself. Pendants
of necklaces were generally
ornamented with amuletic or
religious motifs; a squatting
figure of a king in ceremonial
garb, holding the crook and flail,
is most exceptional.

Placed in a small coffin, like a **shawabty**, this wooden model portrays the shrouded mummy of Tutankhamun on a lion-sided funerary bed. A human-headed bird (**ba**) and a falcon, each with a wing protectively extended over the king's abdomen, represent two forms in which the king might return to his body after death. The model was a funerary gift from Maya, an official who may have saved Tutankhamun's tomb after its early violations by robbers.

Twenty-two black wooden shrines occupied most of the south side of the Treasury. Each shrine had folding doors, tied with a sealed cord. They enclosed figures, usually one or two, enveloped in linen from the neck downward. One of the figures represented Ptah, the patron deity of artists and craftsmen. His cult center was at Memphis, the capital of Egypt when the pyramids were built. His priesthood believed that Ptah had created the world, the gods, and all living beings by uttering their names according to the prompting of his heart. Memphis was sometimes called Hikuptah, "Spirit Mansion of Ptah," which, in its Greek form Aiguptos, "Egypt," became the name of the country. In this gilded wooden figure Ptah is shown wrapped in a garment of feathers and wearing a blue faience skullcap. He holds a **was** scepter with an animal's head and the symbols of "life" and "stability."

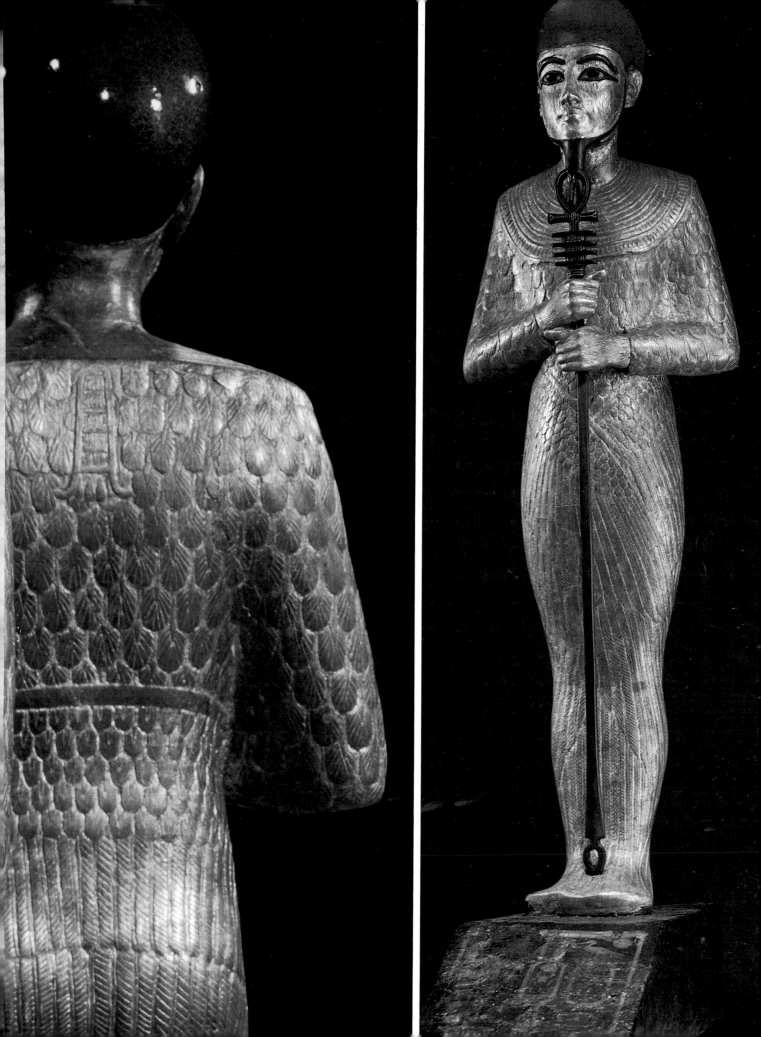

On top of the shrines were four-teen model boats, all with their bows pointing towards the west; there were also other boats, both in the Treasury and in the Annex. The provision in tombs of boats or representations of boats, either painted or sculptured, was one of the most ancient Egyptian funerary customs, and Tutankh-amun included in his tomb models of craft of every known kind, so that he would be able to transport himself wherever he wished to go.

Pages 190–191: Among seven statuettes of Tutankhamun in the shrines were two together, both representing him upon leopards and probably in the underworld. This location is suggested by a scene in a later tomb, which shows Sethy II in the underworld similarly depicted, but upon a lion. The leopard was painted black like all the inhabitants of the underworld, human, animal, and divine, because they lived in darkness except for a brief spell each night when the sun god passed by. The king, being asso-ciated with the sun god, was represented in the golden color of light.

Pages 192–193: Nothing in the dress or the accouterments of this gilded wooden figure of the king indicates its purpose. It is one of a pair from another shrine, both being similar in every re-spect except for the crown. In this figure the king wears the crown of Upper Egypt, a bead collar, a pleated kilt with apron, and san-dals. In his hands are a flail and a long crook, made, like the sandals, of gilded bronze. The deep dip in the front of the girdle, revealing much of the abdomen, is a typical feature of the art of the Amarna period.

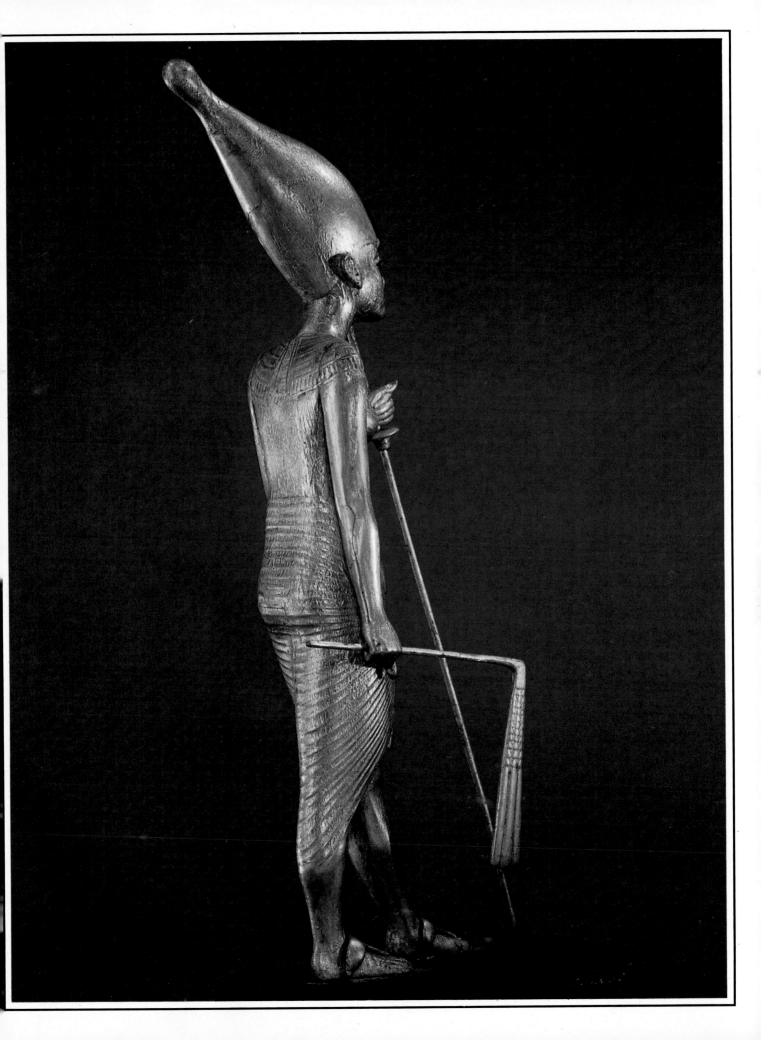

According to a legend, the god of evil, Seth, and his confederates planned to kill the sun god Ra-Harakhty. Hearing about their intention, Ra-Harakhty instructed Horus to attack the enemy. Seth and his confederates, after severe losses in the first battle, transformed themselves into crocodiles and hippopotami. Horus and his followers attacked them with harpoons and were victorious. Every king in his lifetime was the embodiment of Horus; as such he had to keep at bay the forces of evil. The gilded wooden figure at right represents Tutankhamun as Horus throwing a harpoon at one of Seth's hippopotami.

Having neither sail nor oars, this brightly painted
wooden model represents a barge to be towed in a
flotilla, perhaps for transporting mourners and
equipment on the day of the king's funeral. It may,
however, have been intended for his pilgrimages in
the afterlife to sacred places such as Abydos and
Busiris or it may be a relic of an early custom where-
by the bodies of kings were taken to those places
in the interval between mummification and burial.
　The main cabin, with painted representations of
doors and windows, is situated amidships. In the
forecastle and the poop are screens for the crew,
mounted on decks overhanging the gunwales.
Two oars for steering are attached to crutches held
firmly in position by a crossbar in front of the
poop deck.

A shallow box under some of the shrines contained an image of Osiris hollowed out of wood, like a tray with raised sides. Such images, called by the Egyptians beds for Osiris, were placed in both temples and tombs. Those in temples were filled twice a year with soil and sown with grain. When the grain had grown to a height of about ten inches, the image was wrapped in linen, like this example. Through sympathetic magic, the germination of the grain was supposed to impart life to the image and consequently to the dead king as Osiris.

In Tutankhamun's time, funerary figures (this page) resembling mummies, but with the head and neck exposed, were known by the name **shawabty,** perhaps because they were originally made of wood from the persea tree, called in Egyptian **shawab.** Their purpose was to act as substitutes for their deceased owner, or to be his servants, when he was required to undertake agricultural work in the next world. The number buried with one person varied greatly; Tutankhamun had 413. In some tombs there were 401, one figure for each day of the year and thirty-six foremen to control groups of ten figures. This wooden figure, made in the likeness of Tutankhamun holding the crook and flail of Osiris, was a funerary gift from the General Minnakht.

Opposite: An inscription on its pedestal identifies this cobra as Netjer-ankh, meaning "the living god." It is made of gilded wood and was found in one of the black shrines, some of which contained figures of underworld spirits. Illustrations of the underworld on the walls of New Kingdom royal tombs show a serpent which bears the same name, and it is possible that this figure represents that serpent. Netjer-ankh was, however, also the name of one of five serpents depicted with five vultures as amulets on wooden coffins of the Middle Kingdom (about 1850 B.C.), and representations of those amulets in gold were placed in the wrappings of Tutankhamun's mummy. Both being serpents and sharing the same name, they may have had a common origin.

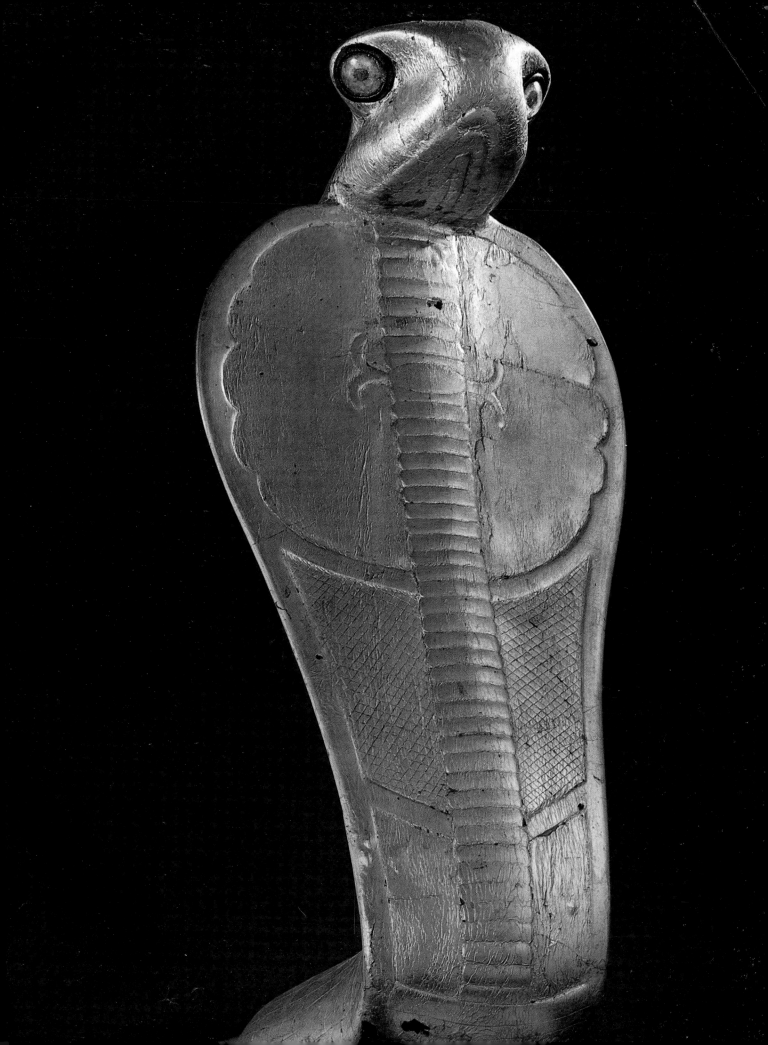

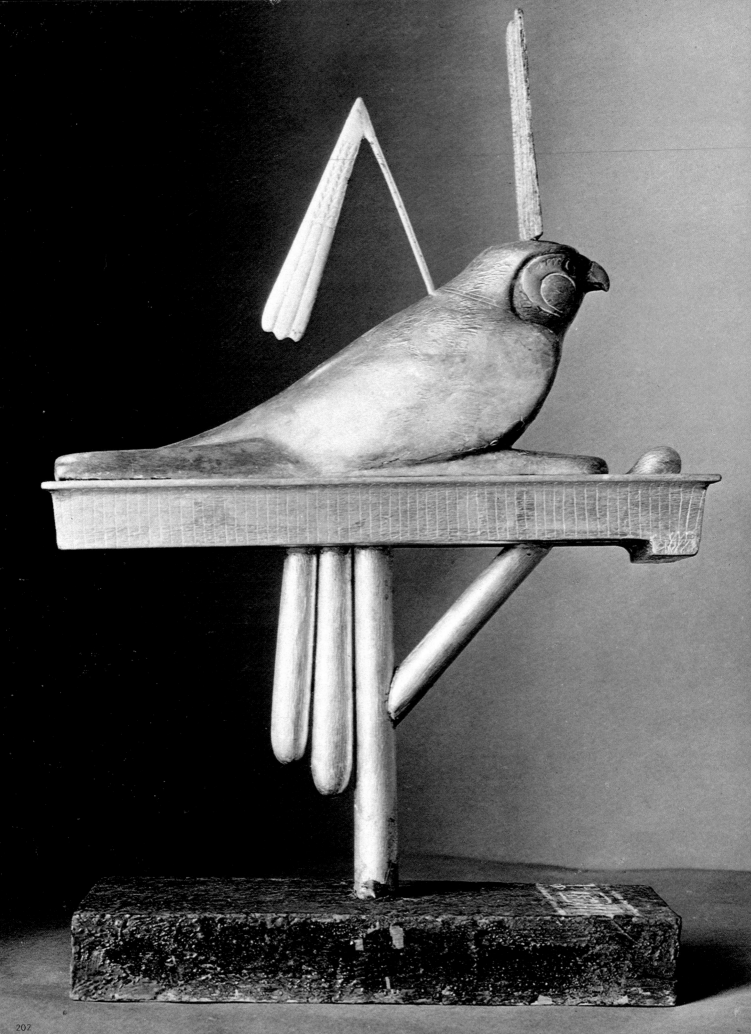

Both these gilded wooden standards are surmounted by falcons, bearing flails and wearing collarettes with counterpoises. Inscriptions on the black pedestals identify them with the gods Sopdu, on whose head are two tall plumes, and Gemehsu. Sopdu is a well-known deity whose cult center was in the eastern Delta. Gemehsu, meaning "he who espies himself," is an old word for a falcon and in late times he bore the epithet "he who gives light with his two eyes." Such standards are generally emblems of districts; if that applies to these two, the district may be Sopdu's in the Delta.

All the representations of chariots driven by
Tutankhamun, whether in warfare or in hunting,
show a bow case attached to the side of the chariot.
This very fine example, made of wood and decorated on both back and front with similar scenes,
belonged to one of the hunting chariots placed be-
side it in the Treasury. The central panel, embossed
in sheet gold, shows the king in his chariot, accompanied by his hounds. The flanking panels,
veneered in marquetry with colored barks, tinted
leather, and gold foil, show the hunted animals
against a background of desert plants. Among the
animals are ibex, oryx, hartebeest, and a striped
hyena, the last being a nocturnal animal and out of
place in this context.

Five years after he first entered the tomb, Carter was ready to begin work on the last of its four chambers, which he called the Annex. Its low doorway lay behind the bed with the hippopotamus heads, and the hole made by the robbers in its blocking had not been repaired by the necropolis staff. The room itself was somewhat smaller than the Treasury. No attempt had been made to straighten the disorder created by the robbers; everything was topsy-turvy, just as they had left it. Their footprints could be seen on the white lid of a bow case (visible in this photograph) and their finger marks on some vessels whose contents of precious unguents they had poured into more portable waterskins. The diverse character of the objects which the eye could see at a glance was quite bewildering; even more than the Antechamber, it gave the appearance of having been merely a storeroom.

Gold and silver apart, the chief objectives of the ancient robbers were the precious oils and unguents, of which about 105 U.S. gallons (400 liters) had been put in the tomb. Thirty-four alabaster vessels, which had held most of these perfumes, were found in the Annex, nearly all of them empty. A small residue remaining in this flask could not be identified. The bands on the neck consist of inlaid blue faience and white limestone imitations of lotus petals hanging from strings made of black and white glass; they represent garlands used to decorate vases on festive occasions.

Two different games could be played on this box-shaped board, which is mounted in a rebate on an ebony stand and is itself veneered with ebony. On one side there are thirty squares inlaid with ivory, five of which are inscribed, for a game called **senet.** The game played on the other side was called **tjau,** "thieves"; it has only twenty squares, three of which are inscribed. Playing pieces, either knucklebones or casting sticks, were kept in the drawer at one end of the board. Hardly anything is known about the rules of the games.

According to a popular myth, the universe was created by the separation of the sky, personified by the goddess Nut, from the earth, personified by the god Geb. The separation was brought about by Shu, the personification of air, who knelt on the earth and raised the sky. It was an action which had to be maintained continuously, otherwise the sky would collapse and chaos would return. This ivory headrest depicts Shu performing the action. Over each of his shoulders is slung the hieroglyphic sign for "protection." The lions, carved almost in the round, symbolize the two mountains on the eastern and western horizons between which the sun rose and set.

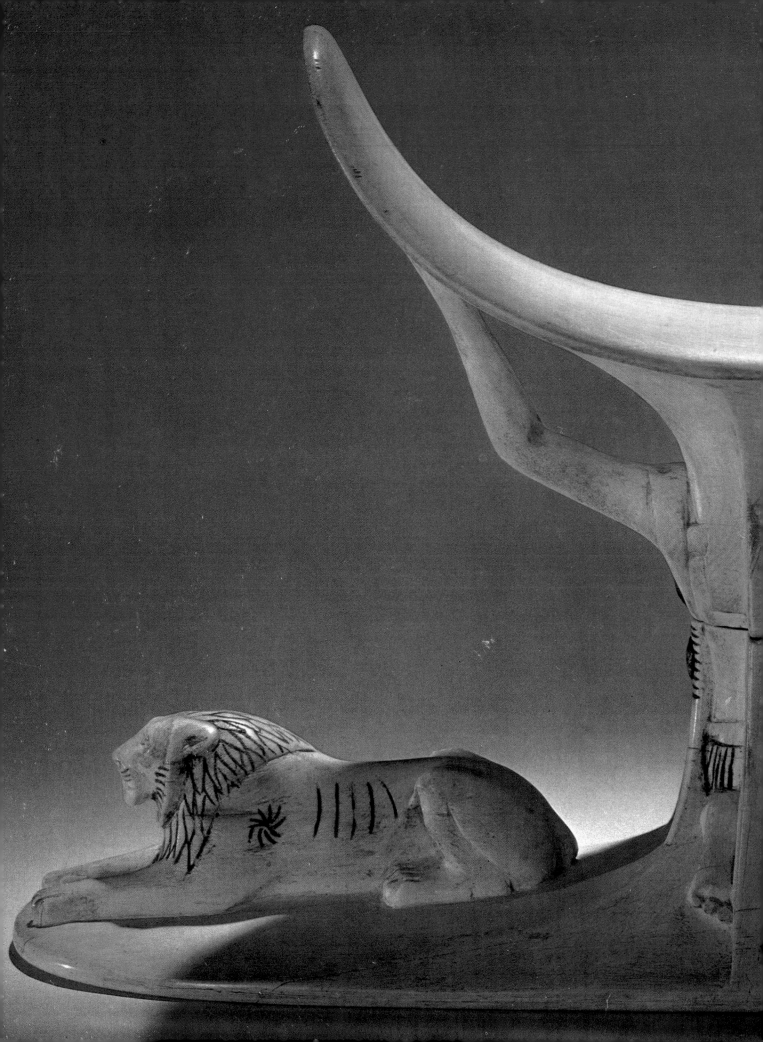

The ancient Egyptians re-garded the head as the seat of life; it was therefore of par-ticular importance for the continuance of existence after death. Magic, however, was needed in order to enable it to function and its aid could be secured through a headrest, either model or real. Tutankh-amun had four real headrests and one model, made of iron—a very rare metal at that time—which was in his mummy wrappings. A magic spell writ-ten on some headrests identi-fies them as Shu; the deceased owner would thus have a supply of air constantly be-neath his head. Another spell attributes the power of resur-rection to a headrest.

About forty objects are visible in this stack, piled up against the wall on the left of the entrance to the Annex. In the foreground is the white bow case shown earlier before the objects in front of it had been removed. The most prominent object is a bed – one of six in the tomb – lying on its side at the top of the stack. Beneath its frame are two broad stretchers, curved so that they would remain clear of the webbing if it should sag under the weight of the occupant. The largest of the objects stacked on the left of the bed is the so-called ecclesiastical throne, and on the floor beneath it, although concealed from view, is an alabaster vase in the form of a bleating ibex. Also on the floor, but on the right, are a lion unguent vase and an alabaster boat. All these pieces will be illustrated in the following pages.

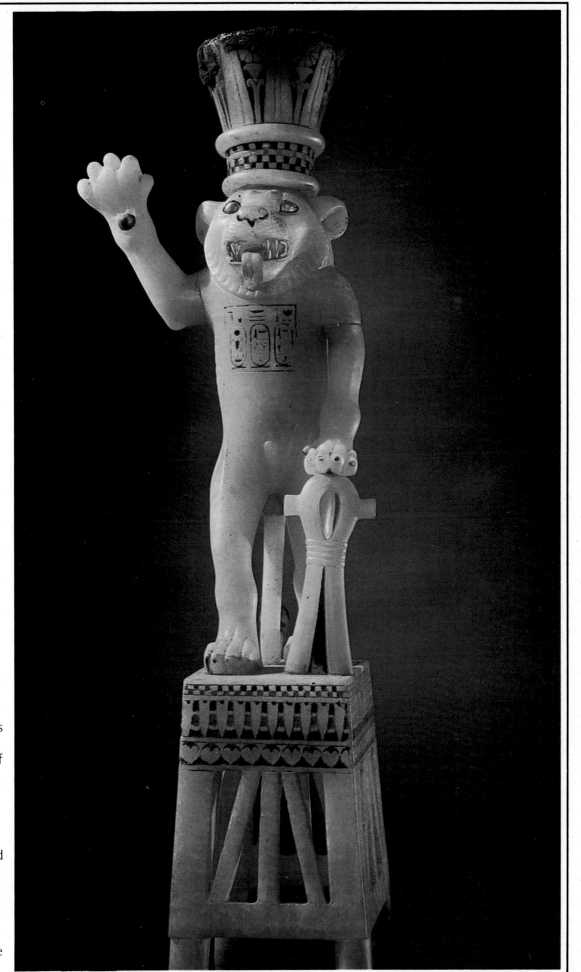

Unguent jars often embodied figures of Bes, a domestic deity associated with pleasures and usually represented as a bandy-legged dwarf with ears, mane, and tail of a lion and sometimes wearing a lion's skin. This unguent vase was probably carved in the form of a lion with floral crown because of the animal's connection with Bes. Standing upright on a pedestal, the lion has gilded eyes and teeth and tongue of ivory, the latter protruding and stained red. The left paw rests on the hieroglyphic sign for "protection." The names of the king and queen are inscribed on the chest.

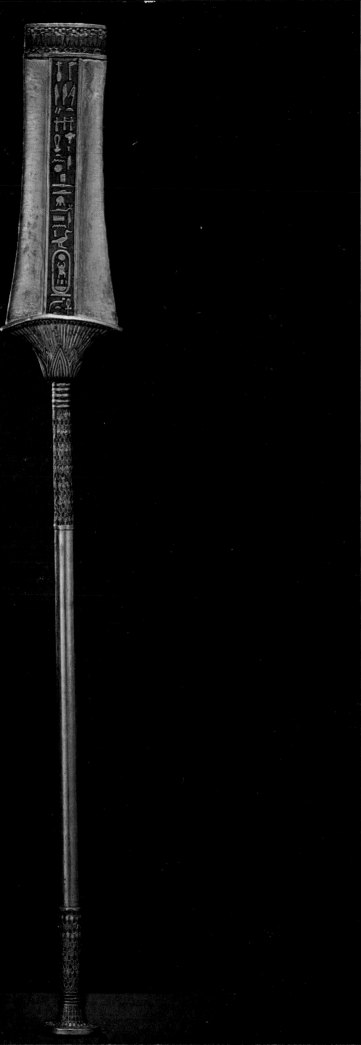

This royal scepter (left) is made of sheet gold beaten on a wooden core. The handle represents a papyrus flower and stem with a feather-pattern design at each end, inlaid with carnelian, turquoise, lapis lazuli, feldspar, faience, and glass. On the side of the blade shown in this picture is a line of inscription reading "The good god [i.e. Tutankhamun], the beloved, dazzling of face like the Aton when it shines, the son of Amun, Nebkheperura, living for ever." Above the inscription is a frieze of lotus petals. On the other side of the blade are rows of trussed and slaughtered bulls.

Opposite: Like the lion shown on the previous pages this recumbent ibex served as an unguent vase. It is carved in alabaster, apart from the red-stained ivory tongue and the one surviving real horn. The other horn, the beard, and the mouth of the vase were not discovered. The eyes, set in copper or bronze sockets, are painted behind glass. Paint has also been used for the various markings and the hooves, and for the royal cartouche on the shoulder. The sculptor has enhanced the naturalistic effect by showing the mouth slightly open and projecting the tongue, to give the impression that the ibex is bleating.

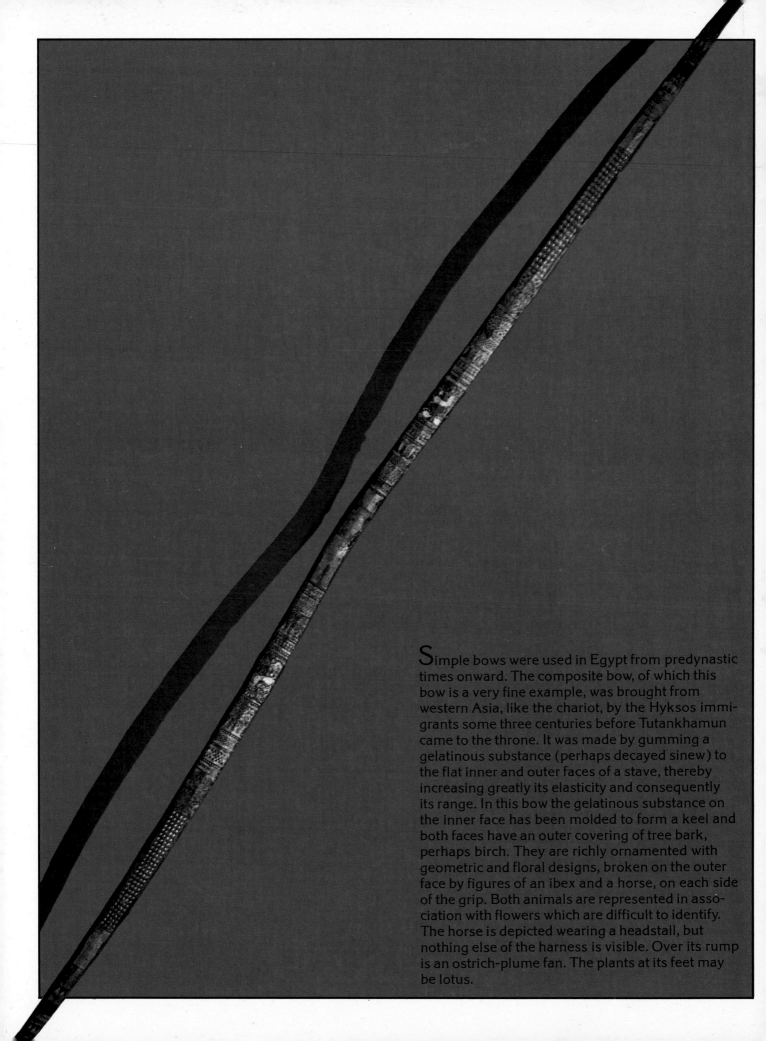

Simple bows were used in Egypt from predynastic times onward. The composite bow, of which this bow is a very fine example, was brought from western Asia, like the chariot, by the Hyksos immigrants some three centuries before Tutankhamun came to the throne. It was made by gumming a gelatinous substance (perhaps decayed sinew) to the flat inner and outer faces of a stave, thereby increasing greatly its elasticity and consequently its range. In this bow the gelatinous substance on the inner face has been molded to form a keel and both faces have an outer covering of tree bark, perhaps birch. They are richly ornamented with geometric and floral designs, broken on the outer face by figures of an ibex and a horse, on each side of the grip. Both animals are represented in association with flowers which are difficult to identify. The horse is depicted wearing a headstall, but nothing else of the harness is visible. Over its rump is an ostrich-plume fan. The plants at its feet may be lotus.

This alabaster model still remains unexplained fifty years after its discovery. It measures twenty-eight inches in length and consists of a tank with a high central pedestal supporting a boat ornamented with ibex heads at the prow and stern. Amidships is what appears to be an open sarcophagus under a canopy whose columns have capitals in two tiers, representing the papyrus and white lotus. Steering the boat is a nude female dwarf and a second nude female kneels on the foredeck and holds a lotus. Carter thought it was a palace ornament; others think that it depicts a princess and her dwarfish duenna sailing for pleasure, or that it was a receptacle for oils or flowers.

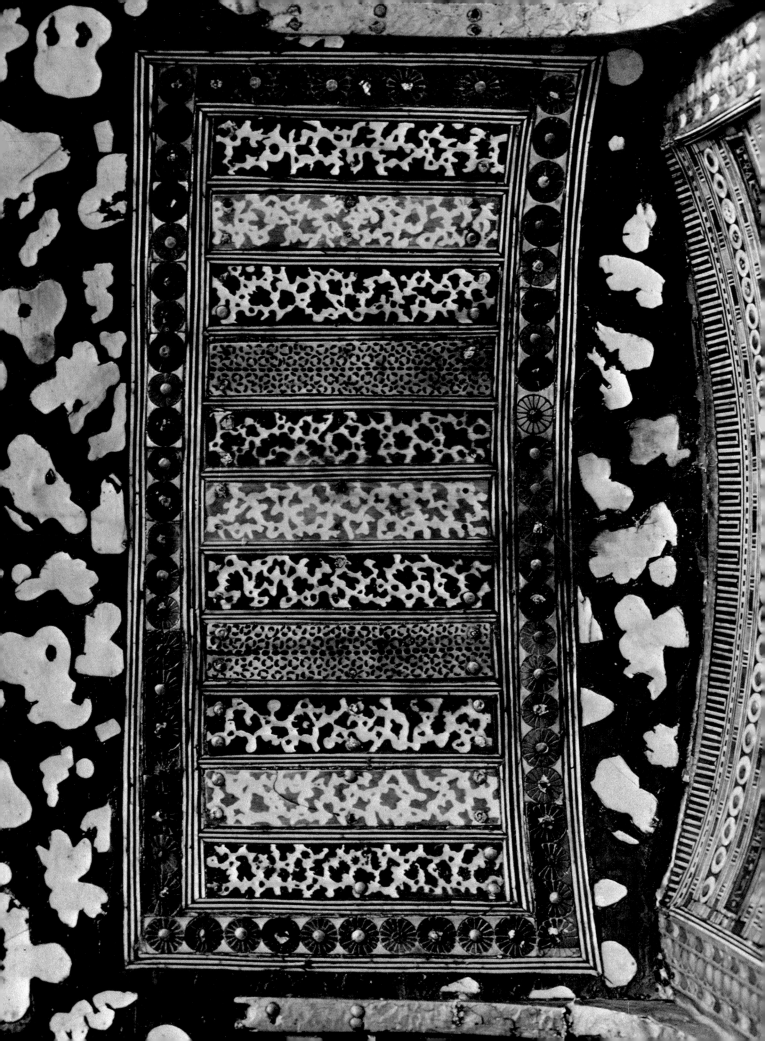

For richness and intricacy of design, the back of this throne – called the ecclesiastical throne from its resemblance to bishops' faldstools in cathedrals – is an outstanding example of Egyptian craftsmanship. Set in sheet gold, the inlay consists of semiprecious stones, colored glass, faience, and ivory. The inscriptions give the king's name in both its early and its late forms, Tutankhaton and Tutankhamun, and another relic of the Amarna period is the large disk of Aton on the top crossrail. The seat and legs, of ebony embellished with sheet gold, resemble the model folding stool in the Antechamber, with the addition of a gilded grille damaged by the ancient robbers. The inlaid ivory panels on the seat are stained to imitate animal skins.

Carter's method of recording the positions of objects before removing them can be seen by comparing this illustration with the similar one shown earlier. Before anything was touched, the expedition's photographer, Harry Burton, photographed the whole mass of objects as they lay on the floor of the chamber. A boldly printed number was then placed on each object within reach and a second photograph was taken, this time of the objects with their numbers. When they were removed from the tomb, all the major pieces were rephotographed individually and details recorded on cards, often with pencil drawings.

The largest object in the picture is an ebony bed overlaid with thick sheet gold. It has carved lion's legs with drums under the paws, a woven mesh covering, and a footboard ornamented with elegant floral motifs (see below). Single stems and flowers of papyrus are draped over the board dividing it into three panels. In the center is the emblem of the unification of Upper and Lower Egypt, papyrus and lotus tied to the hieroglyphic symbol for "unification." The flanking panels are decorated with large clusters of papyrus and perhaps red-tipped sedge, bordered on the out-side with bouquets composed mainly of papyrus and lotus.

The stool in the lower right corner of the picture at left is upside down and partly between the bed and the wall, where it had been thrown by the ancient robbers. Overleaf: Its most striking feature is the gilded grille with the emblem of the unification of Upper and Lower Egypt on all four sides. The papyrus flourished in the Delta marshes and the artist has suggested this setting by showing the stems emerging from leaves at the base, whereas the corresponding element beneath the lotus stems represents a plot of land divided by irrigation canals, the canals being the natural habitat of the lotus in Upper Egypt.

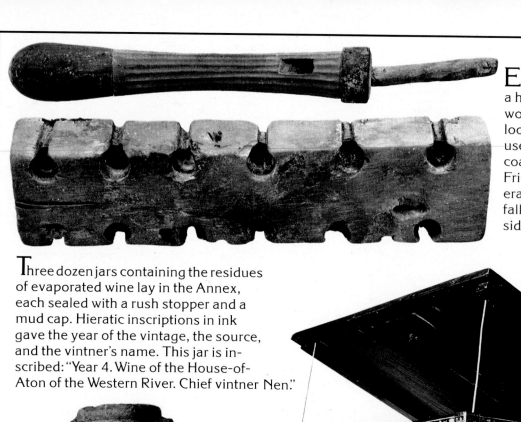

Egyptian fire drills consisted of a hollow handle, a stock, and a wooden bit. A bow with its string looped round the stock was used to rotate the bit in a cavity coated with resin in the hearth. Frictional heat was thus generated and burning wood dust falling through a slot in the side of the hearth ignited tinder.

Three dozen jars containing the residues of evaporated wine lay in the Annex, each sealed with a rush stopper and a mud cap. Hieratic inscriptions in ink gave the year of the vintage, the source, and the vintner's name. This jar is inscribed: "Year 4. Wine of the House-of-Aton of the Western River. Chief vintner Nen."

486

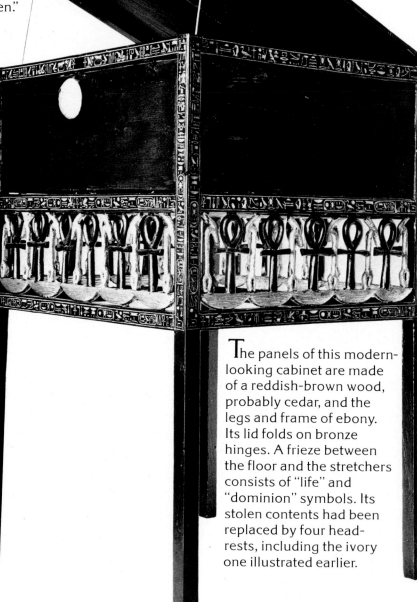

The panels of this modern-looking cabinet are made of a reddish-brown wood, probably cedar, and the legs and frame of ebony. Its lid folds on bronze hinges. A frieze between the floor and the stretchers consists of "life" and "dominion" symbols. Its stolen contents had been replaced by four headrests, including the ivory one illustrated earlier.

Made in three sections and connected by bronze hinges, the traveling bed shown above has two additional pairs of legs in the center which fold inward when the bed is not extended. The footboard consists of plain wooden slats. Both the wood and the linen string web are painted white. The feet rest on bronze drums.

More than a hundred finely woven rush baskets were found in the Annex. The bottle-shaped example at lower left contained dried grapes.

This sling of plaited linen thread (below, center) was found in a box of toys. When the stone was ejected, one cord was held in the fingers and the other released.

One of a pair, the linen glove at the right is tapestry woven in a scale pattern with a border of lotus buds and flowers at the wrist.

Twenty-five faience vases, all except one blue in color, were found in a badly damaged box. This vessel was one of them. It belongs to a type called **nemset,** which is often shown in ritual scenes placed on a stand or an altar. The spouts vary in shape; this one may be a copy of an original in copper. When used for pouring out libations, the lid was removed.

The pomegranate was brought to Egypt from western Asia as a result of the campaigns in Palestine and Syria of the kings who ruled more than a century before Tutankhamun. The Egyptians quickly adopted it, but continued to use its Semitic name (**rimmon** in Hebrew). Models of it were produced in glass, faience, ivory, and other materials, including silver, the material of this vase. The upper part is decorated with bands of petals and the body with cornflowers and perhaps vine leaves.

Eight slender vases, of a kind called **hes,** were found in the same box as the vessel shown in the plate on page 232. They belong to a type which was regularly used both in libation ceremonies and for ritual lustrations. They were made of many different materials, but the commonest was faience, the material of which the three illustrated here are made. Invented in predynastic times, faience consisted of a core of powdered quartz heated until it fused into a compact mass and then coated with glass. The blue or green colors were obtained by copper compounds.

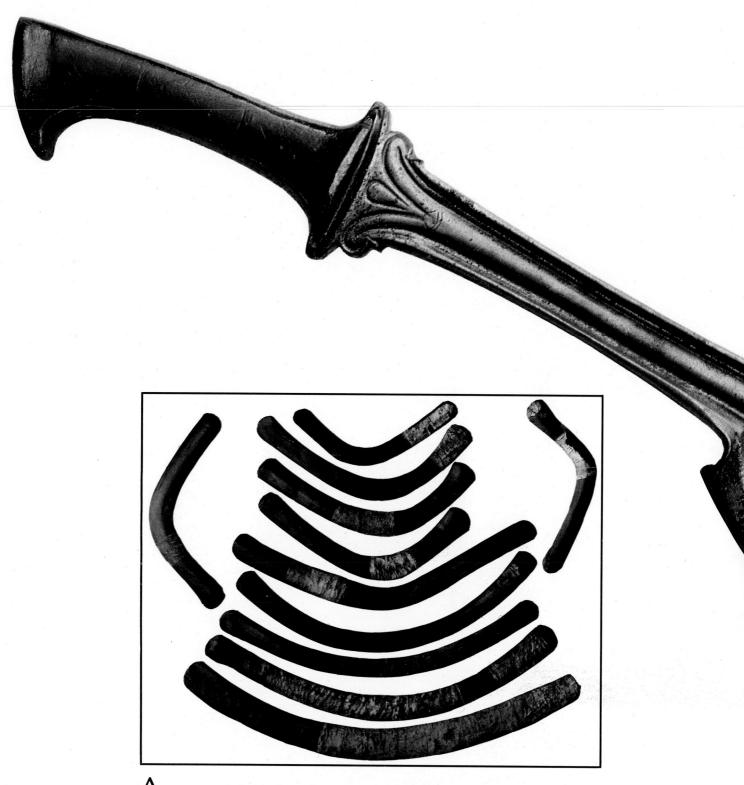

A magic spell dating from five centuries before the time of Tutankhamun promises the deceased that the waterfowl will rise by the thousands as he passes by in his boat in the next world, and when he directs his boomerang at them a thousand will fall. Throwing sticks had the advantage of longer range, but the disadvantage of not returning to the thrower. Both kinds of missile are shown in the small illustration above.

The blade, shaft, and handle of this bronze scimitar are cast in one piece and the handle is fitted with side plates of ebony. The cutting edge, which was on the convex side, has never been sharpened. As a weapon the scimitar was a late arrival in the Egyptian armory, very probably from western Asia. In the New Kingdom kings were presented with scimitars, supposedly from the gods, as a magical pledge of victory.

This openwork shield is made of wood and covered with gilded stucco. It is a ceremonial shield with a heraldic device depicting the king holding two lions by the tail and in the act of slaying them with his scimitar. Above him is the winged disk of the god Horus of Behdet and protecting him from behind is the vulture of Nekhbet wearing the crown of Upper and Lower Egypt. Between her outspread wings is the symbol of "infinity." The action takes place on the hieroglyphic sign for "foreign land," whose inhabitants, the foes of Egypt, are symbolized by the lions. In an eulogistic inscription on the right, Tutankhamun's might and valor are likened to those of Mont, the god of war.

Statues and statuettes of Tutankhamun from the tomb show him wearing golden sandals. These sandals are made of wood and overlaid with a marquetry veneer of bark, green leather, and gold foil on a stucco base. The outer soles are covered with white stucco. The straps over the insteps are of bark ornamented with a diaper pattern in gold foil. On the inner sole are figures of Negro and Asiatic captives bound with stems of lotus and papyrus. Above and below are groups of four bows which, together with the captives, represent the nine traditional enemies of Egypt whom the king symbolically trod underfoot when wearing the sandals. The device had a long history dating back more than a thousand years.

Both these damaged circlets (above, right) consist of beads threaded on bronze or copper hoops. The upper circlet, when complete, had two beaded hoops. The white beads are made of alabaster, inlaid with quartz or transparent glass backed with a red pigment. Probably the black beads are also made of glass and inlaid with gold. The circlets may have been either headbands or collars.

The objects at the right may be anklets but are more probably bracelets. The upper ring, made of crystalline limestone inlaid with lapis lazuli bordered with gold wire, corresponds in shape with gold rings awarded by the king for distinguished services. The lower ring is made of ivory and inlaid with a bronze or copper plate inscribed with the king's name.

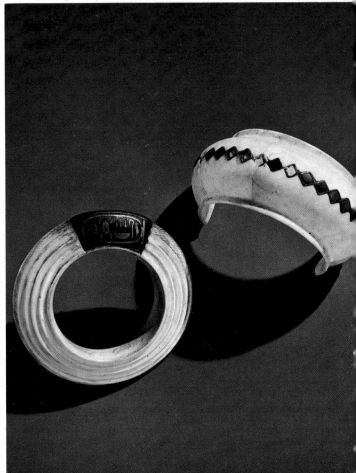

Almost all the smaller objects in the northern end of the Annex were woven rush baskets, with here and there a wine jar lying among them. At the back, however, were some boxes, two of which proved to be of particular importance, one (No. 547) for what it contained and the other (No. 551 and its lid, No. 540) for its qualities as an outstanding work of art. This second box is described in the following pages. Box 547 yielded the double circlet shown earlier and also part of a cap, a headrest, a bracelet, and a gold ornament, but its most exceptional feature was a tall stand fixed to the floor of the box and designed to support a royal headdress. It was the equivalent of the old-fashioned hatbox.

In design this chest resembles a cabin-shaped shrine, except insofar as the main dimension is horizontal and not vertical. It is made of wood and veneered with ivory. Carved in relief and colored on the lid and sides are scenes which are among the outstanding artistic masterpieces of the tomb. Each scene is bordered by garlands and other floral elements set within a frame of red and blue plaques separated by black and white plaques composed of strips of ebony and ivory.

The king and queen are shown in a style reminiscent of the art of the preceding Amarna period. Perhaps the most striking difference is that Akhenaton and Nafertiti are generally represented participating almost as equal partners in the performance of some activity, whereas the role of Ankhesenamun tends to be rather subservient, that of an intimate companion who attends to Tutankhamun's needs.

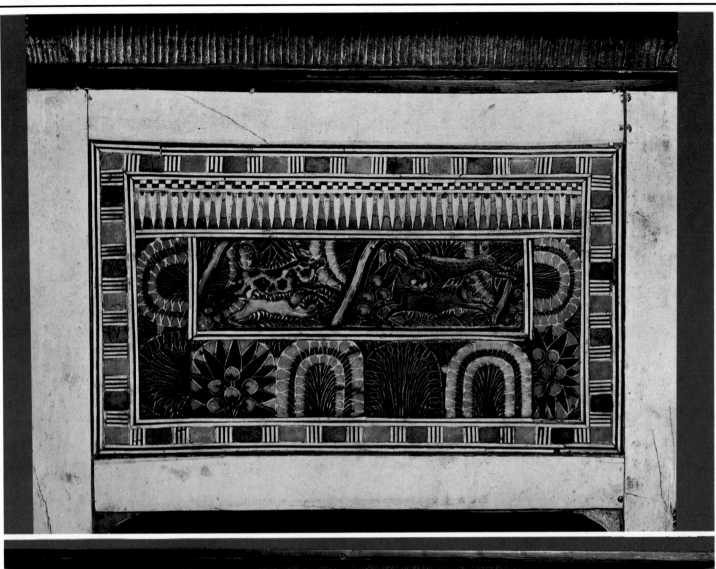

The difference in portraying the relationship of the royal pair between Amarna art and the art of Tutankhamun is well illustrated in the scene carved on the lid of the chest, which Carter rightly described as the unsigned work of a master. It is set in a bower, richly bedecked with flowers, mostly in festoons. The posts which support the vine-covered roof are decorated with circular floral frills, spaced at intervals apart, open poppies arranged in spiral fashion, and, at the top, clusters of papyrus, lotus, and poppies. Under the bower the king, leaning lightly on a long staff, is in the act of stretching his hand to receive two bouquets of lotus, papyrus, and poppies from the queen. In contrast with the relaxed pose of the king, her bearing is erect but graceful and mobile. She is the devoted companion, seeking to give the king pleasure, but nevertheless ministering to him.

The same theme, but
in a different envi-
ronment, is again dis-
played in a scene at
one end of the chest
which depicts Tutankh-
amun shooting with
bow and arrow wild
fowl and fish from the
bank of a rectangular
pond. He is seated
on a curved-back chair
with a cushion and
his feet rest on a cush-
ioned footstool. His
extended left arm hold-
ing the bow is pro-
tected by an archer's
leather bracer from
injury through friction
caused by the string.
The queen sits on a
cushion in front of him,
holding a lotus flower
in her right hand and
an arrow, ready to pass
it to the king, in her
left hand. Beneath the
pond is an attendant
carrying a fish and
a duck, both trans-
pierced by one of the
king's arrows. The
whole scene portrays
the idyllic setting for
the king's afterlife.

When work was discontinued for any length of
time, the staircase was refilled, and re-excavated
when Carter was ready to resume. Risk of
theft was not the only reason for this precaution.
Perhaps once in twelve years violent rainstorms
turn the Theban ravines and valleys into raging
torrents. Tutankhamun's tomb, in the foreground
of the picture at the right, would have been
quickly flooded if such a cataclysm had occurred
when it was open. As an additional precaution,
a removable watertight cover of timber was made
to block the outer doorway. In the event, Carter's
safeguards were never put to the test. Paradoxi-
cally, however, the survival of the tomb and its
preservation from further robbery in antiquity
may have been largely due to such a deluge,
soon after it was resealed by the necropolis
guards, which left a deposit of mud over the floor
of the Valley, thus making its entrance
indistinguishable.

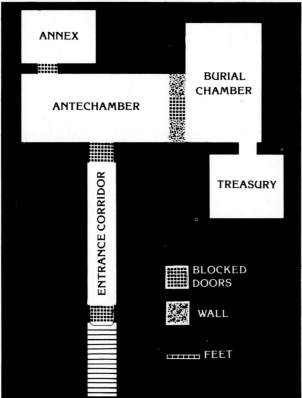

ANNEX

BURIAL
CHAMBER

ANTECHAMBER

ENTRANCE CORRIDOR

TREASURY

▦ BLOCKED
DOORS

▨ WALL

▭ FEET

Carter's procedure in removing the objects from the tomb has been mentioned in the descriptions of previous illustrations. These pictures show three stages in the operation. In the first, Carter and his assistant Callender are bringing the body of one of the state chariots on a padded stretcher up the staircase of the tomb. The second picture shows Alfred Lucas (seated) and Arthur Mace carrying out the same examination as they conducted on every object and applying chemical treatment. All the objects were packed in wooden boxes, usually wrapped in cotton wool and cloth, but some of the most fragile were laid in bran. Lastly, the boxes were placed in stout packing cases for transport by Carter's railway to the riverbank (right).

The Valley and the riverbank were separated by more than five miles, and Carter had only a few lengths of railway track available, which necessitated lifting and relaying the track as the trucks advanced. To add to his difficulties, much of the terrain was rough and there were steep gradients, but the journey was safely accomplished, with the aid of a gang of fifty men, in fifteen hours. On arrival at the riverbank the boxes were loaded on a steam vessel, provided by the Antiquities Service of the Egyptian Government, and seven days later they reached the Cairo Museum. A few objects, including the gold mask and the gold coffin, were taken by train to Cairo, but nearly all the rest went by river. Tutankhamun's mummy, enclosed in the outermost coffin and the stone sarcophagus, was, however, left in the tomb, where it has remained to the present day.

TABLE OF DIMENSIONS

INDEX